THE MYSTICAL LIFE
OF JESUS

▽

JESUS, THE ARYAN GENTILE

The Mystical Life of Jesus

By

H. Spencer Lewis, F. R. C., Ph. D.

*Imperator of the Rosicrucian Order for North and South America,
Fellow of the Essene Ashrama in India, and American
Legate of the G. W. B. Monastery in Tibet*

ROSICRUCIAN LIBRARY
VOLUME III

Martino Publishing
Mansfield Centre, CT
2015

Martino Publishing
P.O. Box 373,
Mansfield Centre, CT 06250 USA

ISBN 978-1-61427-910-5

© *2015 Martino Publishing*

Cover Design Tiziana Matarazzo

Printed in the United States of America On 100% Acid-Free Paper

The
Mystical Life
of Jesus

By

H. Spencer Lewis, F. R. C., Ph. D.

Imperator of the Rosicrucian Order for North and South America,
Fellow of the Essene Ashrama in India, and American
Legate of the G. W. B. Monastery in Tibet

ROSICRUCIAN LIBRARY
VOLUME III

SUPREME GRAND LODGE OF AMORC
Printing and Publishing Department
San Jose, California

First Edition, 1929

Printed and Bound in U. S. A.
THE ROSICRUCIAN PRESS, LTD.
San Jose, California

DEDICATION

▽

To the

Chebaliers of the Militia

in the large party of
men and women from all
parts of North America who accompanied my family and myself in
our long and tedious journey through
Palestine, Egypt, Italy, Turkey, Greece, Switzer-
land, France, Germany, and England, in
search of Holy Shrines and the verification of the facts known to us
through our years of joint
study and research
THIS BOOK IS DEDICATED
as a Souvenir of our Holy
Mission and our Illumi-
nation in the year
1929.

CONTENTS

▽

The Author's Expedition Party in Egypt

A Scene in Ancient Galilee, the Gentile Community
in Which Mary and Joseph Lived

Mount Carmel and the Monasteries

INTRODUCTION

∇

It is a fact that very often *truth* is far more interesting than *fiction*. It is particularly so in regard to the life
of Jesus. Perhaps it is due to the Cosmic Cycle through
which man is passing, or perhaps it is due solely to
man's intellectual development, but man has become
more interested in the life of the Great Redeemer than
he has been in any other period since the dawn of
Christianity.

In my contact with seekers for spiritual truths, cover-
ing twenty-five years, I have found that inevitably the
student of mysticism, metaphysics, psychology, and
occultism, is drawn to a more minute and analytical
study of the life and teachings of the Christ, Jesus. His
whole career, His doctrines, parables, miracles, and
illuminating inferences, gradually fascinate and attune
the spiritual side of each mystical student, and he becomes restless until he fathoms the mysteries of His life.

Why there are any mysteries in the life of Jesus is
revealed in chapters of this book. After many years of
careful study and research, even to the extent of visiting
the Holy and mystical places of Europe, Palestine, and
Egypt, I am still unprepared to say whether the Holy
Fathers who authorized the incomplete, partly errone-
ous, and greatly veiled life of Jesus as it appears in the
Christian Bible, were justified in their actions or not.

Certain it is, not all are prepared even today to comprehend, nor apprehend, the mystical significance of
most of the mysteries associated with pristine Christianity. That there are thousands, perhaps several millions,
now ready for the *truth* is undeniable; but even so, they
are but a small fraction of those who have accepted and
found Peace and Salvation through the offerings of the
Christian Church.

To those who in orthodox sincerity will reject much
that is presented in this book, I can say only: "Hold fast
to that which is good!" If your faith, your knowledge,
and your conviction in regard to Christian matters
serves you well, and there is no inner urge to look beyond the veil, then do not do so. Permit nothing to
weaken or lessen your adoration and worship of Him
who is your Saviour and your Lord.

To those who believe that a more intimate knowledge
of Jesus, the *Son of God*, the Master, the Avatar, and
the Mystic, will endear Him to their hearts, and to those
who feel that the inner-self needs *more light* on the mysteries of His mission, I present the Chapters of *The
Mystical Life of Jesus* as a comprehensive survey of
things long held in seclusion by a few, but now deserv-
ing of wider circulation.

The story of the life and mission of Jesus as presented
in this book makes no sectarian appeal. I know, as a
fact, that the Jesus revealed herein is acceptable to as
many Jews as Gentiles, to as many Roman Catholics as
Protestants; and in these days of religious controversy

and profound concern regarding the growth of the numberless thousands who do not attend any Church and who seem to be losing their interest in religious matters, I am happy to say that I know that thousands will find in this book a key to their problem and an incentive to re-read the Christian Bible and reconsider their rejection of the Church.

I said I *know* these things. Through my official capacity I am in daily contact with many thousands of such persons in North America, and thousands in other lands. In my public lectures throughout the United States for twelve years, in personal interviews with the spiritually restless among the populace, and in journeys to foreign lands, I have seen the effect of these truths. Parts of the chapters in this book have been used in public discourses, some of the interesting facts have been used in private lessons, and others have been presented in personal conversations. The result has always been an awakening of interest in the life and teachings of Jesus, and generally a happy realization that Jesus and His Doctrines were wholly acceptable in the newer revelations.

In the past few years, certain pamphlets have appeared claiming to contain hidden facts regarding the life of Jesus. In most cases these stories contained such improbabilities or inconsistencies as to condemn them as fabrications. Several of the most popular of these have claimed that they were the result of a *discovery* of some rare manuscript or record hitherto hidden in a secluded monastery. The real origin of all that was dependable in such pamphlets was the uncovering of certain Holy books of the ancients as did contain casual references to incidents in the life of Jesus rejected by the Holy Fathers when the first versions of the Bible were authentically compiled.

The facts contained in this book are not drawn from any newly discovered manuscripts, writings, or records. In fact, it cannot be said that the facts contained herein are new to either the Holy Fathers of the early Christian Church, to the most profound and analytical writers of spiritual subjects, or to the most advanced of mystics in many lands.

The Rosicrucian archives in foreign lands, embracing the records of the Essenes, the Nazarenes, and the Nazarites, as well as the complete records of the Great White Brotherhood in Tibet, India, and Egypt, have always been sources of knowledge for the worthy inquirer into the history of all Avatars and especially into the history of Jesus. It is from this dependable source that all the facts contained in this book have been drawn —not at one time and not without years of labor and indefatigable study and service.

Wherever possible, verification or substantiation has been secured from the writings and records of the early Church Fathers, historians, or archivists. Extracts have also been taken from the writings of Jews, and even from the so-called heathens, whenever possible. Such citations are plainly indicated.

I wish to take this opportunity to thank all those who in past years have carefully examined portions of my writings on this subject and have called my attention to additional points which should be covered. I wish also to thank those members in my tour to the Near East during the months of January, February, and March of this year, who acted as my companions in my special researches, and aided my secretary and myself in se-curing the information needed to give a personal veri-fication to the important statements contained in this book. It was a glorious work and I hope that each of these many companions will find some reward for his efforts in the book which I have dedicated to them.

H. Spencer Lewis

Egyptian Temple,
Rosicrucian Park,
San Jose, California.
April 15, 1929.

▽   ▽   ▽

CHAPTER I

THE MYSTERY OF THE ESSENES
▽

EFORE one can properly understand and appre-
ciate the history and real story of the birth and
life work of the Master Jesus, one must have
an understanding of the ancient organizations
and schools which contributed to the preparation for His coming.

Within the last hundred years, a great many notations in sacred literature have been discovered relating
to the Essene Brotherhood and the activities of this
organization in Palestine just prior to and during the
lifetime of the Master Jesus. Many of these notations
have verified the references to the Essenes by such
eminent historians as Philo and Josephus, and have explained many of the mysterious references found in the
sacred writings of the Hebrews as translated in the
Christian Bible.

The possible relationship of the Essene Brotherhood
to the early Christian activities has not only aroused
the interest of hundreds of eminent churchmen and
Biblical authorities, but it has caused one question to be
asked by thousands of students of mystical literature:
"Why has the history or story of the Essenes been withheld from general knowledge?"

The answer to this question is simply that there was
a desire on the part of those who knew the story to keep
the Essene Brotherhood shrouded in mystery for the

purpose of protecting its work and teachings from being publicly discussed and eventually criticized and scoffed at by those students or professors of orthodox Christianity who have labored so diligently in the past to make even a greater mystery of Christ and Christianity.

The Rosicrucian records have always been replete with satisfactory and extensive details of the history and activities of the Essene Brotherhood, and no initiate of the Rosicrucian Order, or, in fact, no profound student of the ancient mysteries who became worthy of contact with the ancient records was ever left in ignorance regarding the Essenes. There is no reason why the veil should not be drawn aside, and some of the facts regarding the Essenes revealed to the world today because of the advancement that has been made in the study of occult literature, and the broad-minded view that is taken by the average educated student of spiritual and mystical subjects. It is for this reason that I feel justified in giving the following facts in regard to the Essenes.

In the first place, it probably will be sufficient in this brief outline of their organization to say that the Essenes were a branch of the illuminated brotherhood or Great White Lodge, which had its birth in the country of Egypt during the years preceding Amenhotep the Fourth, Pharaoh of Egypt, and the great founder of the first monotheistic religion, who supported and encouraged the existence of a secret brotherhood to teach the mystic truths of life.

The several mystic schools of Egypt, which were united under one head constituting the Great White Brotherhood, assumed different names in different parts of the world, in accordance with the languages of each country, and the peculiarities of the general religious or spiritual thought of the people. We find that at Alexandria, the members of the Brotherhood there assumed the name of Essenes. Scientists have speculated considerably in regard to the origin of this word and its real meaning. So many unsatisfactory speculations upon its root have been offered in the past that there is still considerable doubt, in the minds of most authorities, regarding it. The word truly comes from the Egyptian word *Kashai,* which means "secret." And there is a Jewish word of similar sound, *chsahi,* meaning "secret" or "silent"; and this word would naturally be translated into *essaios* or "Essene," denoting "secret" or "mystic." Even Josephus found that the Egyptian symbols of light and truth are represented by the word *choshen,* which transliterates into the Greek as "Essen." Historical references have been found also wherein the priests of the ancient temples of Ephesus bore the name of Essene. A branch of the organization, established by the Greeks, translated the word Essene as being derived from the Syrian word *asaya* meaning "physician," into the Greek word *therapeutes,* having the same meaning.

The Rosicrucian records clearly state that the original word was meant to imply a secret brotherhood, and while most of the members became physicians and healers, the organization was devoted to many other humanitarian practices besides the art of healing, and not all of its members were physicians in any sense.

The spread of the organization into the many lands near Egypt was slow and natural, in accordance with the awakening consciousness of the people; and we find that the Essene Brotherhood became a very definite branch of the Great White Brotherhood representing the outer activities of the G. W. B., which was primari-ly a school of learning and instruction. Thus, for several centuries before the dawn of the Christian Era, the Essene Brotherhood, as an active band of workers, maintained two principal centers, one in Egypt on the banks of Lake Maoris, where the great Master Moria-El the Illustrious was born in his first known reincarnation, educated, prepared for his great mission, and established the principle and law of *baptism* as a spiritual step in the process of initiation. The other principal center of the Essene Brotherhood was first established in Pales-tine, at Engaddi near the Dead Sea.

Going through the Rosicrucian records pertaining to the Essenes, I find thousands of notations regarding these two branches, and from them I have selected the following statements as being the most interesting and most definite in their connection with the mystical life of Jesus.

The branch in Palestine had to contend with the despotism of the rulers of that country and the jealousy of the priesthood. These conditions forced the Essenes in Palestine to hold themselves in greater silence and solitude than they had been accustomed to in Egypt. Before they moved from their small buildings and sacred enclosure at Engaddi, to the ancient buildings on Mount Carmel, their principal activity seemed to be the trans-lation of ancient manuscripts and preservation of such traditions and records as constituted the foundation of their teachings.

It is recorded that when the time came for them to move from Engaddi to Mount Carmel, their greatest problem was the secret movement of these manuscripts and records. Fortunately for us, they succeeded in pre-serving the rarest of the manuscripts that came out of Egypt, and in other ways preserved the ancient, tradi-tional stories and teachings. It is from these that we derive most of our knowledge regarding both the Essenes and the Great White Brotherhood. A picture of how they lived, and what they believed and taught, un-doubtedly constitutes a story of intense interest to all modern students of mysticism and sacred literature.

Every member of the Essenes in Egypt or Palestine, or of the *Therapeuti*, as they were called in other lands, had to be a pure-blooded descendant of the Aryan race. This point is very important in connection with the facts that will be revealed regarding the birth and life of the Master Jesus. Likewise, they were students of the Avesta writings, and adhered to the principles taught therein, which laid great stress upon a healthy body and a powerful mind. Before any qualified Aryan could become an *Adept* in the Essene Brotherhood, he had to be prepared in childhood under certain teachers and instructors, raised with a healthy body, and had to be able to exercise certain mental powers under test. Every adult applicant who was allowed to partake of the daily meal in the Brotherhood building, was assigned at the time of his initiation to a definite mission in life, and this mission had to be adhered to regardless of all obstacles, and all temptations, even to the sacrifice of his life. Some chose to be physicians or healers, others artisans, teachers, missionaries, translators, scribes, and so forth. Whatever worldly things they possessed at the time of their initiation had to be donated to the common fund, from which all drew only as was needed. The simple life they led, free from any indulgence in the pleasures common to the public, made it unnecessary for them to draw upon these funds except in rare instances.

Immediately upon initiation, each member adopted a robe of white composed of *one piece of material,* and he wore sandals only in such weather or at such times as was absolutely necessary. Their attire was so distinct or unique that among the populace they were known as the *Brethren in White Clothing.* The term *Essene* was not popularly known, and only the learned knew of it. This accounts for the lack of references to the Essenes in most of the popular histories or writings of the time.

They lived in well-kept buildings, usually within a sacred or well-protected enclosure, in community fashion. All of their affairs were regulated by a committee or council of judges or councilors, one hundred in number, who met once a week to regulate the activities of the organization and to hear the reports of the workers in the field. All disagreements, all complaints, all tests and trials were heard by this council, and one of the regulations indicates that they were always cautious in expressing opinions of one another, or of those outside of the organization, and they were not critical of the lives or affairs of the people they were trying to reform or assist. They also adhered strictly to one of their laws: "Judge not—lest ye be judged also."

It is possible to set forth here their definite articles of faith as recorded in ancient, secret writings. While these articles of faith appear in slightly different words in the various branches of the Essene organization, they are undoubtedly based upon the articles of faith adopted by the Great White Brotherhood at the time of the establishment of the Essene organization.

Number One: God is principle: His attributes manifest only through matter to the outer man. God is not a person, nor does He appear to the outer man in any form of cloud or glory. (Note the similarity of this article to the statement of John IV:24: "God is a Spirit, and they who worship Him must worship Him in Spirit and in Truth.")

Number Two: The power and glory of God's dominion neither increases nor diminishes by man's belief or disbelief; and God does not set aside His laws to please mankind.

Number Three: The ego in man is of God, and at one with God, and is consequently immortal and everlasting.

Number Four: The forms of man and woman are manifestations of the truth of God, but God is not manifest in the form of man or woman as a being.

Number Five: Man's body is the temple in which the soul resides, and from the windows of which we view God's creations and evolutions.

Number Six: At the transition or separation of the soul and body, the soul enters that secret state where none of the conditions of the earth have any charms, but the soft breezes and great power of the Holy Ghost bring comfort and solace to the weary or the anxious who are awaiting future action. Those who fail, however, to exercise the blessings and gifts of God, and who follow the dictates of the tempter and of the false prophets and the ensnaring doctrines of the wicked, remain in the bosom of the earth until they are freed from the binding powers of materialism, purified, and assigned to the secret kingdom. (This explains the ancient, mystical term of "earthbound," referring to those who are still enslaved to material temptations for a time after transition.)

Number Seven: Keeping holy the one sacred day of the week that the soul may commune in spirit and ascend to contact with God, resting from all labors, and discriminating in all actions.

Number Eight: To keep silent in disputes, to close the eyes before evil, and to stop the ears before blas- phemers. (This is the original of the Oriental law, "to speak no evil, to see no evil, and to hear no evil.")

Number Nine: To preserve the sacred doctrines from the profane, never to speak of them to those who are not ready or qualified to understand, and be pre- pared always to reveal to the world that knowledge which will enable man to rise to greater heights.

Number Ten: To remain steadfast in all friendships and all brotherly relations, even unto death; in all positions of trust never to abuse the power or privilege granted; and in all human relationships to be kind and forgiving, even to the enemies of the faith.

Every department of the organization was supervised by stewards, who were in charge of the material things turned into the general fund by every member. This general fund was called the *poor fund,* and was used to relieve the sufferings of the poor in every land. This point reminds us of the statement in Matthew XIX:21: "Sell all thou hast, give it to the poor, and follow Me."

Hospices were established by the Essenes in various communities for the care of the sick and the poor, especially during epidemics of famine or disease. These places were called *Bethseida.* We find in this feature of their work the origin of the hospices and hospitals which became well-known some centuries later. A special staff of workers were connected with these places and these were called Hospitalers. Herein we find the origin of another branch of the Brotherhood which later became a more or less separate organization. The Essenes also established rescue homes in various communities and at the entrance to most cities had a place called a *Gate,* where strangers or those in need of something to eat or guidance would be cared for temporarily. Recent discoveries in Jerusalem have revealed the existence of a *Gate* known as the *Essene Gate.*

The Essenes disliked life in cities, and established themselves in communities of small villages outside of the walls or limits of practically every city where they existed. In such communities each member had his own little house and garden, and those who did not marry lived in a community house. Marriage was not forbidden among the Essenes, as is commonly believed, but their ideals regarding marriage were very high, and only those who were well mated and whose mating was approved by the higher officials were permitted to marry.

Women were permitted to become associate members of the Brotherhood, and in only a few cases were they allowed to enter even the early grades of study of the work. This was not because there was any belief among the Essenes that women were inferior to men in either spiritual or mental capacity, but because the Essene branch of the Great White Brotherhood was strictly an organization of men, to carry on a man's work throughout each community. But sisters, mothers, and daughters of the men in each Essene community were permitted to be a part of the community and become associate members. Those of the women who were not married, and who did not care to marry, often adopted orphan children as their own, and in this way carried on a form of humanitarian work for the organization.

In considering their more private affairs, we find that there were no servants, for servitude was considered unlawful, and each household had to be cared for by the members of the household. Some of the rules and regulations recorded in the Rosicrucian records would indicate that their ideas regarding servants and servi- tude were quite fanatical according to our modern point of view. We must remember that in the days when these rules were adopted, most servants in every wealthy household, or the servants of a king or poten- tate of any kind, were like slaves, and, of course, among the Essenes every man and woman was a free being, and slavery or serfdom of any kind was absolutely pro- hibited. In each community everyone took part in any work that pertained to the entire community, and all had a certain amount of menial work to do. The new initiates had to work in the fields, and at certain times serve at the community tables or in the kitchen and at the tables of the rescue houses.

As with many other branches of the Great White Brotherhood, the Essenes never entered into contracts or agreements which required oaths or any form of writing. It became notorious with them that their word was equal to any agreement or contract in writing. They had a definite set of rules and regulations for their lives, which were well-known by all those with whom they had any dealing, and the highest potentates of the land knew that the Essenes could not be bound by any oaths, but were highly responsible when they gave their word in any promise. Even Josephus, in writing about the Essenes in 146 B. C., stated that the Essenes were exempted from the necessity of taking the oath of al-legiance to Herod. Most certainly they would make no promise in the name of God, nor swear to anything in the name of God, for to them, as with the Jews who inherited the idea from them, the name of God was to be mentioned only in a sacred manner in their temples, and at all other times the name of God was unpro-nounceable. In any disagreement with strangers, the Essenes would pay any price demanded or make any sacrifice requested rather than to enter into any argu-ment or have any strained relationships. It was for this reason that the Essenes were thought well of by the Pharisees, and other sects in Palestine, although these other sects severely criticized the religious practices of the Essenes.

Speaking of oaths, however, I am permitted to give herewith the official oath which was taken by the initi-ates, and which was the only oath they ever admitted. It was given upon their own honor, at the time of entering the final degree of initiation, or what we would call the fourth degree of their advancement into the organization. The oath is as follows:

"I promise herewith, in the presence of my elders, and the Brothers of the Order, ever to exercise true humbleness before God and manifest justice toward all men; to do no harm, either of my own volition or at the command of others, to any living creature; always to abhor wickedness, and assist in righteousness and justice; to show fidelity to all men, particularly to those who may be my superiors in counsel; and when placed in authority, I shall never abuse the privileges or power temporarily given unto me, nor attempt to belittle others by a worldly display of my mental or physical prowess; truth shall ever have my adoration and I shall shun those who find pleasure in falsehood; I will keep my hands clean from theft, and keep my soul free from the contamination of worldly gain; my passions I will restrain, and never indulge in anger nor any outward display of unkind emotions; I shall never reveal the secret doctrines of our Brotherhood, even at the hazard of life, except to those who are worthy of them; I shall never communicate the doctrines in any form, but the one form in which received; I shall not add to nor subtract from the teachings, but shall ever attempt to preserve them in their pristine purity, and will defend the integrity of the books and records of our Order, the names of the Masters, Legislators, and my elders."

After the initiate had reached what we might call the fourth degree and had taken the foregoing obligation, he was admitted to the common table to partake of the one great symbolical meal of the day, at which time meditation and contemplation, as well as discussion of the problems of the work, formed part of the period.

It is interesting to note that all the food used by the Essenes was prepared according to the rules and regulations stated in the old documents, in a scientific but simple manner, and while vegetables and especially many forms of raw foods were used, it is not true that all flesh foods were forbidden. There was never any form of overeating or banqueting, and certainly the rules of moderation in all things pertained to eating and drinking as well, hence there was no gluttony or intoxication.

The Essenes seldom took part in public discussions, and never participated in discussions of religion or politics. They were most often silent when others spoke, and silence seemed to be their motto. They were welltrained in the use of the voice and in making incantations, and knew the value of vowel sounds to such a degree that by training they became very soft spoken, even in ordinary conversation. Because of this they were often known as the *soft-speaking men*.

It is but natural that the Essenes would have developed not only magnetic personalities, accompanied by clean bodies, clean raiment, and clean habits, but they developed such beautiful auras that on many occasions these auras became visible to the profane, and especially mystified the Jews who were unfamiliar with the development of a mystical nature, even though their own religion and traditions contained many wonderful mystical laws which they failed to put into practical application.

It was customary for all Essenes to wash their hands and feet upon entering their own homes or the home of anyone else, and to cleanse their hands and feet before any ceremony and before each daily prayer. In their individual homes the Essenes spent much time before the altar in their sanctums, or in the study of the rare manuscripts and books which were circulated among them according to their degree of advancement. They were particularly well-versed in astrology, elementary astronomy, natural history, geometry, elementary chemistry, and alchemy, comparative religions, mysticism, and natural law.

Those who were the physicians in the organization were evidently a curiosity to the peoples of Palestine who were accustomed to the healing methods of that land, which included the exercising of charms, incantations in high pitched voices, the reciting of weird formulas, the striking of crude musical instruments, and the use of strong drugs. The Essenes spoke softly to their patients, and used certain vowel sounds without any evidence of a formula, and often performed the greatest cures by the simple laying on of hands or by instructing the patient to retire to the silence of his home and sleep while the cure was conducted in a psychic manner.

All Essene Brothers or associate women promised to educate their children in the teachings and principles which constituted the foundation of the Essene belief, and to raise each child within the scope of the organization until the child's twelfth year, when it was accepted on probation, which lasted until the twenty- first year, at which time the males were admitted to the first degree, and generally reached the fourth degree about the thirtieth year. The females were admitted on their twenty-first birthday to associate membership, and remained in that the rest of their lives, if they proved worthy by the manner of their living.

Only an occasional Essene was permitted to preach to the public or perform public miracles, and then never as a matter of demonstration, but solely as a matter of service. Those in the Essene Brotherhood who had lived the greatest number of incarnations, and were therefore the most highly evolved, were selected as their leaders, and, from among these, one was selected during each cycle to go out into the world and organize the work in a new land.

The Essenes looked forward to the coming of a great Saviour who would be born within the fold of their organization, and who would be a reincarnation of the greatest of their past leaders. Through their highly evolved knowledge and intimate psychic contact with the Cosmic, they were well-informed of coming events, and the literature of the Essene Brotherhood and the literature of many countries contain references to the Prophets among the Essenes. Menahim was one of their Prophets who became famous through the prophecy that Herod would reign.

There seemed to be a regulation or an unwritten law among the Essenes that none of their members should be engaged in a daily task that was destructive, but always constructive. Therefore we find that the list of prominent Essenes included weavers, carpenters, vine planters, gardeners, merchants, and those contributing to the good and welfare of the public. There never were any in the organization who were armorers, slaughterers of cattle, nor engaged in any practice or business that destroyed the least living thing.

It must be very apparent to my readers that the Essene Brotherhood would appear to have been one of the sects of Palestine and would have been, therefore, classifiied as such by the Jews and by the governmental authorities. For this reason we often read in newly discovered records a reference to the Essenes as one of the *sects* in Palestine. It would be natural for the Jews to consider the Essenes as a religious organization, instead of a fraternal or mystical one, and certainly an organization opposed to the Jewish doctrines and practices. Under these conditions it would be natural for the Essenes to establish their homes in certain communities where others of the same organization lived, and where they could have that form of neighborly companionship which strengthened their interestes.

These Essenes were not Jews by birth, by blood, or by religion, and were often referred to as *Gentiles,* and we find them classified as *Gentiles* in many of the sacred writings, even in the Christian Bible.

CHAPTER II

THE NEIGHBORS OF JESUS

▽

O FURTHER understand the greatness of the advent of the Master Jesus, one should know something of the people and the conditions of the country in which He was born, and with which He had to contend at the beginning of His Mission.

In the first place, Palestine was not one nation of one language, with interests that held one people in common bonds, but a land of many nations, of many languages, and many diverse interests. It was a country of mixed and hostile peoples, whose interests were not only diverse, but so divided and so opposed that peace and harmony among them was impossible. Those of the Jewish faith were not all Hebrews, and those who were Hebrews were Hebrews through the beginning of a new race which had its origin at the time of the Exodus out of Egypt. Among these Hebrews were many in whose veins was Aryan blood by intermarriage; therefore, there were various castes. Hence among the Hebrews, as among those of the Jewish faith, there were those who would not recognize others in the same faith, and who believed that God had ordained the distinctions which they established.

In the midst of these people there were the heathens, whose temples were rapidly rising, and whose rites and customs were becoming prevalent. To the northeast there were the Nomads, wild people living without restraint or regulation, but the vast majority of the people throughout the northeast were Syrians, Grecians, and heathens. To the east and to the west of Palestine, the Egyptian, Phœnician, and the Grecian rites contended for mastery, and in the very heart of Palestine itself the Greek language was dominant and the Grecian rites prevailed.

In the northern section, known as Upper Galilee, lived people who were known as Gentiles. Tiberius itself was wholly non-Jewish. Gaza had its own deity. Joppa was influenced by a heathen religion, according to the Jews. Cæsarea was essentially a heathen city and, to the Jews, was the symbol of Rome—the Rome of Edom—and was therefore to be destroyed; for Cæsarea and Jerusalem, from the viewpoint of the Jews, could never exist at the same time.

The educated classes throughout Palestine spoke Greek. The language of the tribes of Israel had undergone a great change, and the ancient Hebrew language, as it was called, had given place to the Aramæan dialect, except in the academies and theological schools.

The rabbis of the Jewish religion considered that the only real and true land of Israel was that portion immediately south of Antioch. Yet, strange to say, it was here that the first Gentile church was organized and where we find the first Christian disciples.

Palestine, and especially Jerusalem, was most certainly a heathen district just before the coming of the
Master Jesus. While it is true that the Jewish religion
was well-established, it most certainly did not include
the multitudes, and it did not include all of the highest
rank and power.

Judaism itself was quite a problem at this time. The
Pharisees and Sadducees were the two other largest
sects, if we may be permitted to consider the Essenes
as a *sect* from the Jewish point of view; but the former
two held opposite principles and hated each other, while
the Essenes, of course, could not be a part of either
of them.

There was one common emotion which bound all
these people of Palestine in one universal feeling. The
high and the low, the learned and the unlearned, the
rich and the poor, the heathen, the Jew, the common
person or the ruling ones, united in their intense dislike
for the *Gentiles*.

In the financial world the Hebrews represented the
wealth and influence of the nations; for all money
transactions and great trade dealings were in their
hands. Merchandise from the Far East came through
Palestine by means of Arab caravans and through the
Phœnician ports, where fleets of ships owned by the
Jews and operated by Gentile sailors were ever ready
to convey the wares to other parts of the world. The
Jews as traders and bankers were keenly alive to the
value of this situation; and through their financial in-

fluence had a considerable power in the political world also. They were able to obtain secrets of state, and to secure such positions in the civil and military service of the other Gentile nations as permitted them to manipu' late the intracacies of diplomacy so as to further the interests of the Hebrews.

It must be remembered that the orthodox Jews or Hebrews were intensely Hebraic. To their own they were very hospitable, a trait which they considered a great virtue, and to strangers, especially to the Gentiles, they manifested the very opposite in all actions.

The people living in Jerusalem, which was the most advanced habitation in Palestine, had special agents in, and corresponded with, the important parts of the world; and letters were carried from Jerusalem to many other cities by messengers and by peddlers. The wealthy Jews gave great fortunes for the support and defense of the Jewish faith, and such donations were always looked upon as investments which would bring great returns. The Hebrews had their own rulers in most cities, and were allowed to have the same status as the Romans, or the rights of Asiatic citizens, and the special privileges which they demanded because of having been instructed by their God to enjoy such privileges as *God's chosen people*. Having the status of Romans entitled them to a civil government of their own, independent of the rule of the tribunals in the cities in which they lived. They enjoyed such unlimited religious liberties and exacted such religious privileges as they denied to natives in their own lands who were not of their faith.

The ruling class of the Hebrews made themselves obnoxious to the other citizens in each section of the land by closing their stores on the Sabbath and going about idly in gorgeous attire, with a marked display of contempt and abhorrence for everything around them. It was their desire secretly to convert to Judaism the wives and female relatives of all men of power, in- fluence, and wealth, because through such converts they would influence the men in regard to the interests of Israel, and it was freely predicted that the ultimate aim of the proselyting was to wipe the *Gentiles* out of Palestine.

In the Synagogues, which represented the meeting places of the ruling class of the Hebrews, the separation of the classes was strictly observed, and the women were considered as unprepared for a position in the church. We see the attitude toward women in many passages of the Jewish liturgy used in the Synagogues, where thanksgiving is expressed in the following words: "Blessed art thou, Lord and God, that thou has not made me a women." Women were considered as having no souls, and no degree of spirituality that could be developed, and therefore incapable of ever becoming angelic. It is always interesting to those of the Western World today in traveling through the Oriental coun- tries to find that all the statues of angels are of the masculine sex. This idea of a soulless woman is retained in all Latin languages; for we find that the word "angel" is always of the masculine sex. No rabbi would permit himself to be closeted with a woman in religious discussion, nor to deal with a woman in regard to spiritual matters.

Secretly, or silently, the Jews or the orthodox of Israel resented the fact that the scepter of power had been taken away from Judea, and the chosen people of God subjected to the government of Rome. This was a humiliation which the Jews hoped to see undone. Israel hoped that the day would come when her people would rise in power, and when their "King of Glory" would appear and re-establish the power and kingdom of Israel again.

And thus Israel waited. In silence and with suppressed emotion, the faithful anticipated the coming of the great day.

In my recent journey through Egypt, I felt the same suppressed emotion on the part of the Egyptians. As they moved about in silence with cold, emotionless expressions on their faces, and refrained from speaking of the days that were, and the days that *would* come, one could sense that inwardly there was a great fire burning which wanted only the signal to burst into a conflagration that would sweep throughout the whole country. The Egyptians, too, are waiting now for the day to come when the great power and illumination that resides within their traditions and their secret archives will make them the potent power of their land. Just as one could easily sense the possibility of a great confla-

gration in that land, so one may understand and appre-
ciate the condition that existed in Palestine at the time
of the birth of the Master Jesus. Uneasiness has seized
the people; for they had felt the yoke upon their necks
and they realized that they were being held in bondage
and could stand it but a short time longer.

In a social way, vice and degrading practices had
become popular with the masses, and the moral standard was like unto licentiousness. Intrigue and crime
were found even in the courts of law. The governing
power was divided between the two classes, the nobility
and the priesthood. The nobility sought only gratifica-
tion of the baser senses, trying to keep within the law
only as far as it permitted them to gain their selfish
ends. Most of them professed to be of the sect of
Sadducees. On the other hand, the priestly element, or
the Pharisees, known as the "pure, separate ones," were
constantly warring in their determined effort to secure
power and force strict adherence to the letter of their
laws. The Sadducees were their enemies, especially
when the latter were favored in any way with rank
or position.

The masses were downtrodden, and held in ignorance of the true conditions; but they believed that
there was a possibility of rising above their environment
through the coming of a great leader. It is no wonder
that these persons, mostly unlearned and inexperienced
in the things of life, united with any movement which
promised them freedom from their bondage or an op-

portunity to rise to heights which they sensed in their dream world. Thus, in many ways these uncultured and uneducated ones followed leaders and principles which left them in serious situations and sorely disap' pointed. It was the great hope that the coming of the expected Messiah would change all of the sorrowful conditions, and bring about a solidification and unifica' tion of the people of Israel. How this was to come about, no one knew; and only the pretenders who headed the false movements attempted to explain.

The House of David, out of which the true leader of the people of Israel should come, had long since passed into the hands of strangers. The high priesthood, out of which a great Messiah might come, was Jewish only by profession, being politically Roman and Greek in culture, and by birth anything but of the great House of David. Therefore, the great Deliverer who would lead them out of bondage as Moses had done, could not come through the lineage of those who were at present at the head of the nation, nor could He come through those who were of the priesthood.

One phrase remained in the consciousness of the people: "From among thy brethren I shall raise one who shall guide my people!"

CHAPTER III

THE PARENTS OF JESUS

▽

O PROPER consideration can be given to the birth and childhood of Jesus without first becoming acquainted with the parents of Jesus, and their relationship to the mystical facts involved. Therefore, let me state the first important facts, as proved by our records, and then submit the evidence pertaining thereto.

Jesus was born of *Gentile* parents through whose veins flowed Aryan blood, and in whose hearts and minds had been implanted the teachings of the Essene Brotherhood, as well as the more secret teachings of the Great White Brotherhood. This is the simple, definite statement found throughout the Rosicrucian records.

In the Christian Bible, in the Talmud, and in many reliable works, we find verification of these statements. The parents of Jesus lived in Galilee. There is no possible dispute on this point, and they were therefore Galileans in the full meaning of the term. So our first consideration should be of Galilee and the Galileans.

In St. Matthew IV:15, we read: "Galilee of the Gentiles." Strange as it may seem, the average Bible student gives little thought to this expression, and loses sight of its very important significance. Jesus Himself was called the Galilean. For this reason, we must look upon Jesus as having been classified by His own people, or by the people of Palestine at least, as one who was different from them. This warrants us in investigating the real situation, and discovering why the Galileans were Gentiles, and why Gentiles lived in Galilee.

In I Maccabees 5:14, we read that messengers from Galilee, with torn clothing and in great anguish, came to Judas Maccabæus and reported that "they of Ptolemais and of Tyrus, and Sidon, and all Galilee of the Gentiles, are assembled against us to consume us." And Judas told Simon, his brother, to choose certain men to go to Galilee and rescue the Jews who were in Galilee, that they might not be persecuted by the Gentiles. Simon took three thousand men into Galilee, where he fought many battles with the "heathens," and the Jews living in Galilee with their wives and children were brought safely into Judea.

Here we see at once an intimation of the conditions that existed in part of Palestine, and how the orthodox Jews looked upon the Galileans as being not only Gentiles, and of a different religion and race, but as enemies to their best interests.

The transfer of the Jews living in Galilee referred to above was made in 164 B. C. At about the same time, Judas Maccabæus rescued his brothers who lived among the "heathens" in the north of the country (and east of the Jordan) and brought them all to Jerusalem.

According to this account, and many others, there were Jews in Galilee long after the year 164 B. C.

Therefore, Galilee continued as a nation of *Gentiles* or "heathens" until the year 103 B. C., when Aristobulus, grandson of Simon, and first king of the Jews, forced all those living in Galilee to adopt circumcision and the Mosaic law.

We will see by this that the Gentiles living in Galilee, which included the parents of Jesus, were Aryans by blood, Gentiles by natural religious classification, mystics by philosophical thought, and Jews by forced adoption. In other words, the Gentiles of Galilee after 103 B. C. were forced to adopt circumcision and respect the Mosaic law, and in accordance with this law all children at a certain age had to accept the Jewish faith in a formal way by appearing at the Synagogue for probationary admission to the church. If this combination of circumstances and conditions will be kept in mind by my reader, it will enable him to understand the many strange statements that appear in sacred literature.

In the cuneiform inscriptions of Tiglathpileser, there is reference to the conquest of Galilee, but it is generally misunderstood, as are many of the other statements regarding Galilee, because few know that Galilee is also referred to as the land of *Hamath*.

The same name, *Hamath,* is used in the Old Testament, but it seems that modern students of the ancient writings did not recognize in this word *Hamath* the name of the ancient capital of Galilee. However, let it be known now that *Hamath* is the famous hot springs, half an hour south of Tiberius, on the western shore of the Sea of Galilee.

Often in the Old Testament one may read of the "entrance to Hamath" and it always refers to parts of the northern boundary of Palestine. It is the Wady Alhammans, near Magdala, three miles northwest of Tiberius, where Mary Magdalene was born. In other parts of the Bible we read that the king of *Hamath*, who sent his son to salute David, was a Galilean; Solomon's storehouse or granaries which he built in *Hamath* were situated near the Sea of Galilee.

The true spelling of the name is Hammoth, or Ham-math, the Assyrian form being Hammati, which means "hot springs." Many other quotations could be used to show that Hamath was in Galilee. And we will find by other references that a great many Assyrians were sent to Hamath as colonists, and further reference re-veals that the Assyrians were all Aryans. Even Sargon II tells how he deported the Median chief with kinsmen to Hamath.

It was because of this settlement of Aryans in the vicinity of Galilee, and the resulting race of Aryans in that community, that the Aryans of Egypt who were members of the Great White Brotherhood and of the Essene organization, directed their people to go to northern Palestine, and live on the shores of Galilee and associate with people of their own race. There are also many historical notations in Egyptian records, and especially in the ancient records of the Great White

Brotherhood, to show that there was close communion and intercourse between the Aryans of Galilee and the Aryans of Egypt.

Our records also show that at the time of the birth of Jesus, the Galileans spoke a language which was not Hebrew. The fact has been known among students of sacred literature for several centuries that the Master Jesus spoke another language besides Hebrew, and there are indications that He spoke several tongues. These indications have greatly puzzled the students of sacred literature, and much speculation has existed among authorities in regard to this matter. The common agree-ment among these authorities is that Jesus presented most of His parables and teachings to the populace in the Aramaic language, and they also believe that He used some other language that was not Hebrew. Our records clearly show that He used Greek and Aramaic in His general discourses and conversations, and used Hebrew only when He was speaking to those who did not understand the other languages. Most of His beautifully poetic parables and discourses were in either the Aramaic or the Greek language. We will discuss, later, the manner in which Jesus became educated in the Greek language. We will find the use of these foreign phrases in the words of Jesus, in such verses of the Bible as Mark V:41, Mark VII:34, Mark XIV:36, and in many other places.

The Galilean dialect was a constant source of jest for the Jews. Peter was also of Galilee and of the

Gentile race, and we find in Matthew XXVI:73, that some said to Peter: "Surely thou also art one of them; thy speech betrayeth thee." There are many historical notes that show that the Jews recognized the Galileans by the fact that these Gentiles could not distinguish the various Semitic gutterals.

The foregoing are but a few of the hundreds of facts which might be submitted to show that the parents of Jesus were Gentiles, and of a different tongue than the Jews. This makes us question at once the genealogy which is so exhaustively presented in the Bible in an attempt to show that Jesus was a descendant of the House of David. This genealogy in the Bible is presented in two places by two different authors, and the generations in each table do not agree. But aside from this discrepancy, the genealogy is only an attempt on the part of later admirers and followers of Jesus to make it appear that He was of the House of David, as hoped and prayed for by the Jews. It must be borne in mind that at no time during His lifetime, did Jesus Himself refer to His ancestors or forebears, or intimate to the Jews that He was the Messiah of the House of David whom they had anticipated. And we find nothing in any historical records of a contemporary nature, or among the authentic Jewish records, to show that during the lifetime of Jesus, or even during the first hundred or more years after His time, that the Jews or anyone else believed that He was of the House of David. Just when the genealogy attempting to show such a connection was prepared and introduced in the sacred writings is not known, but it is most certainly a very late addition to the writings.

Now we must deal with another phase of the history of the parents, and of Jesus Himself. In much of the Christian literature, Jesus is referred to as the *Nazarene,* and it is commonly believed that this means to indicate that Jesus was born, or spent most of His lifetime, in Nazareth. It is strange how students of Biblical literature, and especially those who have written so exhaustively on the life of Jesus, and who have presented in their teachings and preachments the picturesque details of His life, have never given proper thought to the title *Nazarene,* or investigated its real meaning. It is assumed by all of these authorities, writers, and teachers, that if Jesus was a *Nazarene,* He must have been of the city called Nazareth, and since He and His parents lived in Galilee, the city of Nazareth must have been in that locality. On the basis of such reasoning, it is generally proclaimed that Nazareth was the home town of the parents of Jesus, and that Nazareth in Galilee was the place where Jesus spent His childhood.

I have been just recently in Nazareth and made exhaustive inquiries, for the purpose of verifying the statements contained in the Rosicrucian records, and probably most of my readers will be surprised to learn that at the time Jesus was born, there was no city or town in the whole of Galilee known as Nazareth, and that the city in Galilee which now bears that name is not only a city of more recent years, but was named and came into existence because of the demand on the part of investigators to find some place that would answer to the name of Nazareth in Galilee.

First of all, we must make plain that the title Nazarene did not imply that the person who bore that title was of a city called Nazareth. The title *Nazarene* was given by the Jews to those strange people outside of their own religion who seemed to belong to some secret sect or cult that had existed in Northern Palestine for many centuries, and we find in the Christian Bible that even John the Baptist was called the *Nazarene*. We also find many other references to persons who were known as *Nazarenes*. In Acts XXIV:5, we find some man being condemned as a mover of sedition among the Jews throughout the world, and called a "ringleader of the sect of the Nazarenes." Whenever the Jews came in contact with one in their country who had a different religion, and especially a mystical understanding of the things of life, and who was living in accordance with some code of philosophical or moral ethics that was different from those of the Jews, he was called a *Nazarene* for the want of a better name.

There was a definite sect called the *Nazarenes,* and we find them referred to in the Jewish records as a sect of *Primitive Christians,* or in other words, those who were essentially prepared for and ready to accept the Christian doctrines. In fact, the Jewish encyclopedias and authorities seem to agree that the term *Nazarene* embraced all those Christians who had originally been born Jews, and who neither would nor could give up their original mode of life, but who attempted to adjust the new doctrines with the old. The Jewish encyclopedias also state that it is quite evident that the Nazarenes and the Essenes had many characteristics in common, and were therefore of a mystical tendency. In fact, the Essenes and the Nazarenes were called *heretics* by the learned Jews, but there is this difference or distinction in the use of the two terms. The Essenes were not as well-known to the populace of Palestine as were the Nazarenes, and seldom was a man called an Essene unless the person was well-informed and knew the difference between the Essenes and the Nazarenes; whereas many Essenes and even those of other sects who lived a peculiar life or who did not accept the Jewish religion were called Nazarenes.

Jerome, the famous Biblican authority, refers to the fact that in his day there still existed among the Jews, in all the synagogues of the East, a heresy condemned by the Pharisees, and the followers of it were called Nazarenes. He said that they believed that Christ, the Son of God, was born of the Virgin Mary, and they held Christ to be the one who suffered under Pontius Pilate and ascended to Heaven. "But," said Jerome, "while they pretended to be both Jews and Christians, they were neither."

Turning to the highest Roman Catholic authorities, we find that the title Nazarene, as applied to Christ, occurs only once in the Douai version of the Bible, and this authority states that the term "Jesus Nazarenus" is uniformly translated "Jesus of Nazareth," but this is a mistake in translation, for it should read, "Jesus the Nazarene." Nowhere in the Old Testament do we find the word Nazareth as referring to a city existing any' where in Palestine, but we do find in the New Testa' ment references to Jesus returning to a city called Nazareth. These references are a result of translating the phrase, "Jesus returning to the Nazarenes" to read, "Jesus returning to Nazareth." The interesting point here is emphasized by the Roman Catholic authorities, for they show that whereas Jesus was commonly re' ferred to as the Nazarene, He was not of that sect at all.

Taking the Jewish and Roman Catholic records to' gether, and comparing them with the information con' tained in our own records, we find that the Nazarenes constituted a sect of Jews who, while attempting to adhere to the ancient Jewish teachings, did believe in the coming of a Messiah who would be born in an unusual manner, and who would become a Saviour of their race. After the ministry of Jesus began, these Nazarenes accepted Jesus as the Messiah, and even accepted the doctrines He taught while still trying to adhere to many of the fundamentals of their Jewish religion. The Jewish records state that the Nazarenes rejected Paul, *the Apostle of the Gentiles*, and that some of the Nazarenes exalted Jesus only as a just man.

There was another term for such heretics among the Jews, and this was "Nazarite." According to the Jewish authorities, the term Nazarite was applied to those who lived apart or separate from the Jewish race, because of some distinctive religious, moral, or ethical belief. The Jewish records state that such persons were often those who would not take wine or drink anything made from grapes, or those who would not cut a hair of their heads, or who would not touch the dead during any funeral ceremony. These same records state that the history or origin of *Nazariteship* in ancient Israel is obscure. They state that Samson was a Nazarene, as was his mother, and that Samuel's mother promised to dedicate him to the sect of Nazarites. The Jewish rec- ords state also that it was common for parents to dedi- cate their minor children to the Narazite sect, and they distinctly say that there are references to the fact that Jesus was said to have been dedicated to the Nazarites while still in the womb. The Jewish records say that St. Luke I:15, refers to this dedication. Helena, the Queen, and Miryam of Palmyra, are mentioned as Nazarites in the Jewish records, and many other persons famous in sacred literature were known to be Nazarites.

That the terms *Nazarite* and *Nazarene* had naught to do with a city or town called Nazareth is plainly indicated by many historical records. We have said that the present town of Nazareth in Galilee received its name because a place had to be found that would fit the common understanding in regard to the village in which the parents of Jesus lived, and where He spent His boyhood. During the first few centuries after Christ, when the Christian doctrines were in the making and the Holy Fathers of the Roman Catholic Church and religious students in general were searching for every historical site connected with the life of Jesus, each spot, place, and incident in the career of this great man was eagerly tabulated and glorified. My recent visit through Palestine made plain to me that this desire to find historical, sacred sites and glorify them has not ended, and will probably continue for hundreds of years. The absurdity of most of this becomes apparent when even the casual tourist discovers that three, four, and five different places are pointed out to him as being the same spot where some particular incident in the life of Jesus occurred.

In searching for a place that would answer to the name of Nazareth in Galilee, great difficulty was experienced, since no such city was mentioned in the Old Testament, and none of the ancient maps of the time of Christ revealed such a site. A very small settlement, however, called "en-Nasira," was found far from the Sea of Galilee, and this was immediately re-named "Nazareth" and associated with the early life of the boy Jesus. The discovery of the town of *en-Nasira* was made in the *third century after Christ,* and since then has been known as the town of Nazareth, but even today it is lacking in any of the evidences which would warrant the use of that name. In Mark VI:1, 2, the statements are made that Jesus went back to His own country and His disciples followed Him, and when the Sabbath day was come, He began to teach in the Syna' gogue. In the fourth verse of that chapter, Jesus re' ferred to the fact that He was a prophet in His own country, among His own kin, and in His own house. These statements have always been taken to refer to Nazareth, the town in which many Biblical students believe Jesus was born and in which He spent His boyhood. Now, if Jesus did return to His home town, and did preach in a *Synagogue to great multitudes,* it could not have been at *en-Nasira,* or the so-called town of Nazareth; for even in the second and third centuries after the birth of Jesus, *en-Nasira* or Nazareth had no Synagogue and was not large enough to have any building in which multitudes could have listened to Jesus, nor were there multitudes in that vicinity to hear Him. So the references in ark to His home town could not refer to *en-Nasira. En-Nasira* was only a settlement around a spring which was at that time called the "spring of the guard house," but I find that now in recent years it has been changed and is called "St. Mary's Well." This change of name and the giving of a religious significance to some unimportant site in Palestine, is typical of the changes that are being rapidly made in that country for the benefit of tourists.

Turning to the old Jewish records, we find these state that only in the books of the New Ttestament, written long after the lifetime of Jesus, is the town of

Nazareth mentioned as a village in Galilee, and that such a place is not mentioned in the Old Testament, in the historical writings of Josephus, nor in the Talmud. During the lifetime of Jesus, the town of Joppa was the important city in the locality of Galilee, and was the one which attracted all tourists and is referred to most often in historical writings.

In the Roman Catholic records, and in their encyclopedias, we find that the town of *en-Nasira* was known as a strictly Jewish village up to the time of Constantine, and is referred to as one being inhabited *wholly by Jews.* Therefore, this little village surrounding a well could not have been the center of the Gentile population of Galilee. At the present time, there is a small church or chapel in Nazareth which I visited, and which is supposed to stand above the grotto in which Mary and Joseph lived at the time that the archangel announced to Mary the forthcoming birth of the incarnation of the Logos.

All of the foregoing facts point out very clearly that Mary and Joseph and the child born to them were considered, along with many others in their locality, as *Nazarenes, Nazarites,* or people of a non-Jewish sect. And the many other references to this sect clearly show that it was one which held religious and mystical views as permitted the acceptance of the fundamentals of the Christian doctrine. Taking this into consideration, we have at once an interesting picture of the conditions existing in and around Palestine just prior to the Christian era. We have, first of all, a large number of men and women, even children, who were either Jewish by birth, Gentile by birth, or of various races and bloods, but who had refused to adopt wholly or completely the Mosaic law, and were Jewish only because the laws of the land forced them to adopt *circumcision,* to appear in the Synagogue when twelve years of age, and to be enrolled as Jews. Yet these persons were mystically inclined in their beliefs, and followed the Jewish teach-ings only so far as they revealed God and God's laws and served them in their study of Divine principles. They were prepared by some school or some system which made them ready to accept the higher mystical teachings as they were revealed from time to time by the progressive minds or by the teachings of Avatars.

On the other hand, there was the one definite organization of mystics known as the *Essenes,* which conducted many forms of humanitarian activities, in-cluding hospices, rescue homes, and places for the care of the poor and needy. The Essenes had their northern center in Galilee, among the Aryans, because they had been directed to this locality by the center of their or-ganization in Egypt, known as the Great White Brotherhood. The Essenes were not popularly known, were quiet and unostentatious in their activities, and were distinguished by the populace only by their white raiment. The *Nazarites,* the *Nazarenes,* and the Essenes mingled freely and undoubtedly sought to carry on their independent activities without interference one with the other, and they unquestionably had many ideals and purposes in common. But the Nazarites and Nazarenes were popularly recognized and known to the populace, and for this reason all who did not accept the Jewish faith, or who were heretical in their Jewish beliefs, were classified as Nazarenes and Nazarites, not as Essenes.

In and around the shores of the Sea of Galilee, lived these people—mostly Gentiles of Aryan blood of the several sects, Nazarenes, Nazarites, and Essenes. They, too, were looking for the coming of the great Master, the great Avatar, the great Messiah, who would not only redeem Palestine but the whole of the world, and bring contentment to Israel and all peoples. These mystics contemplated, with true understanding, the re-incarnation of one of their own great Masters. We must bear in mind that the belief in reincarnation was not only an established belief among these mystics, who were classified as heretics and as Gentiles, but also among the most orthodox of the Jewish people at that time. This accounts for the many references in sacred literature, and even in the Christian Bible, to a great man, a great teacher, as having been *someone else at some other time;* for they believed that the greatest among them were great because of previous preparation, previous existence, and previous attainments. Naturally they looked for the new great Master, the new redeemer of the world, to come out of the past in a new body and as a well-prepared individual of high attainments.

The Rosicrucian records show that not only did each of the homes of these Essenes and Nazarenes and Nazarites have a sanctum, in which daily prayers and solemn meditations were held, but many hours of each day and evening were given to mystical practices and the development of a spiritual power within their beings, which made possible the many miracles they performed and the great work which they did among the poor and needy.

They were well advanced in the understanding of most of the mystical laws which the Rosicrucians and other mystics of the world today study and practice, and they knew the potent power of certain spiritual laws when applied specifically for any definite purpose. To them, such miracles as Incarnations of a highly Divine nature, and the coming of a great leader into their midst, through *uncontaminated material laws,* were not impossible, nor improbable, and they lived a life typical of that which the mystics of today believe is lived by the Masters in Tibet and in parts of India and Egypt.

Joseph was not only a devout Essene, and carpenter by trade, in keeping with the rules of the organization, but Mary, his wife, was an associate member of the organization. Yet both of them had been forced to accept the Jewish church and had identified themselves in a purely formal way with the faith in accordance with the law of the land.

With these facts in mind, let us now approach the interesting subject of the birth of Jesus.

CHAPTER IV

THE IMMACULATE CONCEPTION OF
AVATARS

▽

HIS incident in the life of Avatars is one that is very difficult to approach and more difficult to present to those who have not attained that high degree of mystical understanding and awakening which naturally would bring to the student a spiritual understanding of the conception and birth of Avatars.

I realize fully that the standard Christian story of the Immaculate Conception of Jesus is one that is not accepted by those who reject *any* of the Christian doctrines. In fact, the authorized Christian version of the Immaculate Conception is a very difficult one for the uninitiated and undeveloped mystic to comprehend, and certainly appears to be an impossible story to those who are of an analytical mind, and who do not com' prehend any of the mystical laws and principles as taught by the ancient Masters.

Perhaps I will do better than others who have attempted, in the past, to reduce the mystical phase of the birth of Jesus to a semi-mystical presentation, and perhaps I may fail altogether. I am not limited by any creeds or dogmas which require that I shall adhere to a standardized version; and if I fail to make my reader comprehend, or perhaps *apprehend,* the real mystery of the Immaculate Conception, it will be because I have been limited solely by an inadequate vocabulary to express in general terms that which every mystic understands *inwardly,* and because of the inability of some of my readers to read between the lines of my statements and realize what I cannot reduce to such crude things as printed words.

First of all, it should be understood by those who approach this great mystery with an open and unbiased mind, that Jesus was not the first great Master, Avatar, or *Son of God,* to be "born of a virgin." The authorized Christian version of the Immaculate Conception and birth of Jesus presents the story as though it were unique and exclusively a Christian manifestation. If nowhere else in the history of God's messengers on earth, or the working out of God's plans for the redemption of man in all ages and cycles, there had ever been a similar incident or a similar manifestation of the great mystic powers of the universe, operating as an unusual manifestation of God's omnipotent ways, then the mystery of the conception and birth of this great man would be more difficult to explain and more difficult to comprehend.

To the mystics of the Orient in all lands and of all ages, the great mystery of the Immaculate Conception and spiritual birth of a Son of God is accepted not only as a possibility but as a fact *natural to the life of every great Avatar.* Christians or students of Christian literature in America who are accustomed to hear the mystery of the Immaculate Conception referred to as one of the problems of faith, and one of the doctrinal points upon which the faith of thousands of Christians is broken, are surprised when they tour through foreign lands to find that even those who are not Christians and who are of the Mohammedan, Hindu, Buddhistic, or heathen faiths, find no difficulty in accepting the story of an Immaculate, spiritual conception and birth, and believe that this one feature of the life of the Master Jesus is the only one which is consistent with the claim that Jesus was the great Redeemer and Saviour of the world. In fact, during my recent trip through lands which brought me in contact with persons of Oriental faiths, I found most of them who were not Christians expressing themselves on this subject in this wise: "If you Christians believe that Jesus was a *Son of God,* or the *Divine Appointed Messenger* to redeem any part of the world through the message He had to give, then you must believe that He was divinely conceived and born, for there can be no question of such distinctive birth if He was a Divine Messenger." When I explained to some of them that there were so-called Christians or students of the Christian doctrine who could not accept the idea of Divine Conception and birth, but who still believed that Jesus was a great Master, a Divinely Appointed Messenger, a true *Son of God,* and an Avatar of unusual authority from on high, these Orientals merely smiled and said that such a viewpoint was an absurdity, for—according to their viewpoint — no man humanly conceived and born, could attain any degree of Divine Authority which would make him the Christ of his time.

Thus we see that the great problem resolves itself into a problem not of the *fact* of the Immaculate Con' ception or the Divine Sonship of Jesus, but a problem of human comprehension on the part of the conscious' ness in the Occidental world as compared with the consciousness we find in the Oriental world. In other words, we are face to face with the fact that not the validity of the claim of Immaculate Conception and birth of Jesus should be given serious thought by stu' dents of spiritual mysticism in the Western world, but the lack of understanding and comprehension on the part of those millions who have not yet attained the proper degree of spiritual understanding regarding the spiritual laws operating in such important events.

The Oriental of any of the various faiths points out to us of the Occidental world the fact that we are attempting to struggle with a principle in the spiritual world with which we are least acquainted, and for a comprehension of which we are least prepared. The mystics of all lands agree that until man is prepared, through spiritual development and comprehension of the higher laws, to understand easily and in its sublime fullness, the actuality of spiritual conception and Divine Birth, he is not ready in any sense to understand the teachings and the true message brought to this world by any of the great Avatars, especially that of the last and greatest of them all, Jesus the Christ.

This does not mean that it is impossible for the sincere student of Christian doctrines to comprehend at least the mystical laws involved in the possibility of an Immaculate conception and Divine Birth, but it does mean that such a student must try to see and comprehend the mysticism that is fundamental in all of the Christian doctrines. The Rosicrucians hold the same viewpoint that the Orientals hold in this regard; namely, that the orthodox Christianity in the Western world today too greatly slights the mysticism and mystical principles which are fundamental to Christianity and which constituted the pristine Christianity of ancient times. In other words, too much thought is given to the literal meaning of words, and the material interpretation of all of the principles involved in Christianity, which leaves almost a total neglect of the pure mysticism that makes possible a real understanding or spiritual comprehension of Christianity in its original form.

Added to this is the reluctance on the part of the Occidental world to accept as facts and actual possibilities the so-called miracles of the Bible. I do not agree with such authorities as the late William Jennings Bryan and others who have claimed that the scientific trend of our thinking and our highly scientific education in the Occidental world has tended to blind us to the spiritual truths in the Bible or in all sacred literature.

I do not believe that materialistic science is in any way responsible for the Occidental's inability to understand the higher spiritual statements found in the sacred writings of the Bible, or the other books of other creeds. I believe that this inability on the part of the minds of the Western world is due to the unawakened status of the spiritual side of our natures and the absence, except in the various occult and metaphysical schools of the Western World, of such general teachings along spiritual lines as would properly prepare us for an understanding of that which is accepted readily and understood thoroughly by the Oriental mind.

I have said that we should bear in mind that Jesus was not the first of the great teachers who came as a messenger of God to be born of a virgin, or to have been conceived by Divine Principle. A few references to similar incidents in the past may help my readers to understand what is meant by this statement.

It is a fact that Divine Births and Divine Conceptions were so currently accepted among the ancients that whenever they heard of one who had greatly distin-guished himself in the affairs of men, they immediately classified such a person as having been born of super-natural lineage. Even in the heathen religion, various gods were declared to have descended from Heaven and made incarnate in man. The learned Thomas Maurice, in his unusual book called *Indian Antiquities*, goes so far as to state that "in every age and in almost every religion of the Asiatic world, there seems uniformly to have flourished an immemorial tradition that one god had, from all eternity, *begotten another god.*"

I may add that our own records of ancient traditions and sacred writings contain many references to religious movements in antiquity, in which the great leader was claimed to be "God's Begotten Son."

India had a number of Avatars or Divine Messengers who were Incarnated through Divine Conception, and two of them bore the name of "Chrishna," or "Chrishna the Saviour." Now Chrishna was born of a chaste virgin called Devaki, who, on account of her purity, was selected to become the *mother of God.* In this instance, we find a very ancient story of a virgin giving birth to an immaculately conceived messenger of God.

Buddha was considered and believed by all his followers to have been *begotten* of God and born of a virgin whose name was Maya or Mary. In the ancient stories of the birth of Buddha, as understood by all the Orientals and found in their sacred writings long before the Christian Era, we read how the Divine power, called the Holy Ghost, descended upon the virgin Maya. In the ancient Chinese version of the story, the *Holy Ghost* is called *Shing-Shin.*

The Siamese, likewise, had a god and saviour who was virgin-born, and whom they called Codom. In this ancient story, the beautiful young virgin has been informed in advance that she was to become the mother of a great messenger of God, and one day while in her usual period of meditation and prayer, she was impregnated by Divine sunbeams. When the boy was born, he grew up in a remarkable manner, became a protege of wisdom, and performed miracles.

When the first Europeans visited Cape Comorin, the most southerly extremity of the peninsula of Hindustan, they were surprised to find the natives, who had never made contact with the white races of Europe, worship' ping a Lord and *Saviour* who had been Divinely Con' ceived and born of a virgin.

When the first Jesuit missionaries visited China, they wrote in their reports that they were appalled at finding in the heathen religion of that country a story of a redeeming master who had been born of a virgin and Divinely Conceived. This god was said to have been born 3468 years B. C. Lao-Tsze, the famous Chinese God, was claimed to have been born of a virgin, black in complexion, and described as marvelous and as beautiful as Jasper.

In Egypt, long before the dawn of Christianity, and long before any of the writers of the present Christian Bible were born, or any of its doctrines conceived of as Christian, the Egyptian people had several messengers of God who were born of virgins through Divine Con' ception. Horus was known to all the ancient Egyptians as having been born of the virgin Isis, and his Concep' tion and birth was considered one of the three great mysteries or mystical doctrines of the Egyptian religion. To them, every incident in connection with the Con' ception and birth of Horus was pictured, sculptured,

The serpent was used as a mystical symbol in the early sacred writings of various schools of religion, and very often used as an emblem of the "Word" or "Logos." In this sense it became the symbol of the *tempter* in the fall of man. The serpent was also the emblem of the Holy Ghost or the Power that impregnated the life in the virgin. In this sense it was the incarnation of the "Logos." The emblem shown above represents the serpent as found engraved or carved on many an-cient monuments to represent the "Logos." The Ophites also venerated this same symbol as an emblem of Jesus the Christ.

adored and worshipped as are the incidents of the Conception and birth of Jesus among the Christians today. Another Egyptian god called Ra was born of a virgin. I have seen on one of the ancient walls of a temple along the Nile, a beautifully carved picture representing the god Thoth—the messenger of God— telling the maiden, Queen Mautmes, that she is to give birth to a Divine *Son of God,* who will be the king and Redeemer of her people.

Turning to Persia, we find that Zoroaster was the first of the world redeemers acclaimed to have been born in innocence through the Immaculate Conception of a virgin. Ancient carvings and pictures of this great messenger show him surrounded by an aura of light that filled the humble place of his birth. Cyrus, king of Persia, was also believed to have been of Divine origin, and in the records of his time, he was referred to as the *Christ or the annointed Son of God,* and was considered as God's messenger.

Even Plato, who was born in Athens, 429 B. C., was believed by the populace to have been a Divine Son of God by a pure virgin called Perictione. It is recorded in the ancient records that the father of Plato, who was known as Aris, had been admonished in a spiritual dream to hold pure and sacred the person of his wife, until after the Divine Conception and birth of the child that was to come, and that this child's conception would be by Divine means.

Apollonius, who was still living and performing great miracles and teaching in various lands during the early part of the life of Jesus, was also born of a virgin mother, according to the stories that were recorded of him during and shortly after his time. According to these stories, the mother of Apollonius in 41 B. C. was informed by a god in a dream that she would give birth to a great messenger of God who would be known as Apollonius.

Speaking of famous miracle workers and teachers who left behind them unquestioned records of great work in behalf of mankind, we find that Pythagoras, who was born about 570 B. C., had Divine honors paid to him through and after his lifetime. According to the sacred writings about him, his mother conceived him through a *spectre,* or the *Holy Ghost,* which appeared to her. His father, or foster father, was also informed through a vision that his wife was to bring forth a son through Divine Conception, and that the son would become a benefactor to mankind.

The story of Aesculapius is very interesting. He became a great performer of miracles, a messenger with a Divine message for all mankind, and was considered a true *Son of God.* When the Messenians sought to learn of the birth of Aesculapius, they consulted the oracle of Delphi, and were informed that an invisible God or *Holy Ghost* of the Divine Kingdom was his father, that Coronis was his earthly mother, and that he was born at Epidaurus. According to the story, when

Coronis experienced the sacred event of Divine Conception, she sought to conceal her pregnancy from her
father because she did not believe that she could make
worldly men understand the strange occurrence. So
she went in hiding at Epidaurus, where the child was
delivered months later in a lowly and humble goat
stable, on a mountain side. A herder of goats, by name
Aristhenes, going in search of a goat and a dog missing
from his fold, discovered the young child in the stable
and would have carried him home, had he not seen,
when approaching the child, that its head was encircled
with fiery rays which told him that the child was a
Divine Being. His report of the finding of the child
spread throughout the land, and the people from all
quarters flocked to the stable to pay homage to the
Son of God, and brought valuable presents which they
laid at the feet of the infant. The child was honored
as a god not only in Phoenicia and Egypt, but the
worship of him passed into Greece and Rome.

Even on this side of the great ocean, the tribes of
North and South America had gods that were supposed
to have been Divinely born. Long before the landing
of Columbus, the inhabitants of ancient Mexico worshipped a saviour and world redeemer whom they
called Quetzalcoatle, who was born of a pure virgin
according to the traditions which the holy fathers, who
came with Columbus, discovered in the ancient writings
carved on the walls of the temples. According to the
story, then long established, a messenger from Heaven

had announced to his mother that she would bear a son by Divine Conception, and that he would be the saviour of the world. There was an established Mexican hieroglyphic which conveyed the story of the Divine Conception and birth of this Mexican god.

The Mayas of Yucatan also had a virgin-born god, corresponding with Quetzalcoatle, whose name was Zama; and he was termed "the only begotten son of the Supreme God."

In Nicaragua, Peru, Guatemala, and other countries, there were other Divinely Conceived and uniquely born gods.

I think I have shown, in just these few out of the many hundreds of well-recorded instances, that among the Orientals, and especially among those people whose religion had a well-developed mystical basis, the idea of Immaculate Conception or Divine Birth was not an improbability, but a well accepted possibility.

It has been said by many of the critics of the story of the Immaculate Conception of Jesus, that if Jesus had been conceived and born as stated in the Christian records, it is strange that none of the contemporary writers, none of His disciples, not even Jesus Himself, ever referred to this fact during His lifetime, and that only many years after His passing did the story of His Immaculate Conception and birth become established. This sort of argument would be sound and reasonable only if the Immaculate Conception and birth was unique with Jesus, or in other words, if He had been the first and only great messenger of God to have been considered of Divine origin and birth. But if we consider that it was common belief among the peoples of the Oriental lands, and of Egypt and Palestine, that every great messenger, every Avatar, every Son of God ordained by Divine decree to raise the status of the peoples of his time was born of Divine Conception, then we can understand why in the case of Jesus, neither His disciples nor the writers of history considered the event of such outstanding importance as to write about it, enthuse over it, or make of it the *unusual miracle* that the Christian church makes of it today.

In tracing back the very complete records of the ancient pre-Christian Avatars and Sons of God that greatly influenced the development of civilization, we find in the Rosicrucian records and in some other writings that are fragmentary, that the disciples and followers of each of these Avatars or messengers devoted more time and thought to the recording of the sayings, teachings, and demonstrations of the Avatars than to the recording of the events connected with their *births and transitions.* Even in the score or more cases where the Immaculate Conception and Divine Birth of these pre-Christian Avatars in various lands is recorded, the statements are brief, concise, and very often merely incidental to the story being told. The facts of the Immaculate Conception and births are disposed of hurriedly as though they were of secondary importance, and to be taken for granted by the reader of the life of each of these Avatars. In no case do we find that the disciples and followers of the Avatars considered the Immaculate Conception and birth as a feature for adoration and worship, as we find in the case of the Christian teachings today. Very often the statements in regard to these miraculous births were made as briefly as we, at the present time, refer to the fact that some great man was born on such and such a date, with the assumption that every person *is* born, and *must* be born at *some place* in a manner in keeping with his race and the conditions of the country in which the event occurred.

I am sure that when these facts are taken into consideration, those who have heretofore been puzzled because so few historical references can be found in ancient writings regarding the Divine Conception and birth of Jesus, will realize that they have been seeking for something that, from the Oriental point of view, was not the outstanding or important event of His life. It is a fact that among the Orientals the lives and teachings and practical demonstrations of the teachings on the part of these Avatars were considered all that was important about them, and the incidents of birth and location of birth, and of their ultimate passing, were points to be considered only by those intimately associated with the Avatars, and were recorded merely for the purpose of completing the record.

The next important point to have in mind is the fact that the reason for the general acceptance by mystics of the fact of Divine Conception lies in the common belief among the mystics and Oriental philosophers that the power of thought or the power of a mental or audible *word* is capable of impregnating matter and bringing lifeless matter into consciousness. If we try to assume that the impregnation of matter in a mystical manner like this is an unusual miracle of doubtful nature, never having been proved, and not acceptable except on the basis of unfounded faith, then we must also assume that all the fundamental teachings of the mystics of the Orient, and all of the claims made in occult and mystical literature by competent teachers and by men whose fame and integrity have been well-established, are false, unfounded, unreliable, and unworthy of our consideration. And if we assume this, then there is little hope for us in the teachings that come from the Orient, and little reason for us to believe in the superior power and hidden, secret principles of Divine energy. The mystics of all ages have claimed, and through the so-called miracles have proved to themselves, that certain latent, potent principles can be invoked by man and are applied by God in the creative processes of the universe. The very creation of the world itself is considered by all the mystics of the Orient as the first great demonstration of the potency of the *Logos,* or the power of the *Word* breathed into space where no life existed, resulting in immediate impregnation and the manifestation of living matter. The mystics of the Orient rightfully contend that in the beginning all non-living matter was impregnated with life by a Divine process, without the application of material laws. No other conception is possible to their understanding or acceptable to them. And if the first great impregnation of life in this manner is accepted, why should there be any question of lesser demonstrations in the case of an individual being, or the impregnation of a *single cell of life?*

Mystics of all times have demonstrated that even the spoken word, composed of a properly intoned vowel uttered by man, has the power to disturb the status of matter, and to set it into vibration or to change its elementary nature or its chemical composition. In demonstration of this, mystics of the Orient—and some highly evolved ones of the Occident—have learned how to utter a sound, or to produce a sound upon a violin string or other musical instrument, which would cause a manifestation in matter. It is common with the Rosicrucians and with mystics of other schools who have learned how, and who have developed to the proper degree of perfection in these things, to utter vowel sounds or, by mental concentration, direct invisible, potent energies to such focal points as would cause a manifestation in non-living and living matter. It is the aim and ambition of millions of students of mystical law to attain that degree of perfection where they can perform seeming miracles of this kind. To these mystics and to the rational mind comprehending the laws involved, it would seem that if man is capable of applying these mystical principles in such a manner as this, it certainly would not be *improbable*, let alone *impossible*, for the Mind of God to have directed certain powers to impregnate matter and bring about not only the Immaculate Conception with which we are dealing in this chapter of the book, but many similar manifestations of an unusual nature.

Therefore, the Rosicrucian of evolved understanding and the mystic of spiritual attainment, readily and understandingly accepts the Immaculate Conception of Jesus, and sees in it no violation of natural or spiritual law, nor any exception to truly scientific principles.

Those who cannot accept the Immaculate Conception and Divine Birth of the Master Jesus are probably laboring under the limiting comprehension of materialistic consideration, and have not attained a spiritual development in their evolution which makes possible the comprehension and apprehension of the higher laws.

There is but one point upon which the Rosicrucians and the mystics of the Orient disagree with the *Fundamentalist or strictly orthdox* of the Christian church, and this is in the *uniqueness* of the Conception and birth of the Master Jesus. The Christian doctrines teach that Jesus was the *only* begotten Son of God, and the only instance where the Word was made flesh, and where God sent upon the earth a Divine Son to redeem the world. The Rosicrucians understand that Jesus was *not* the first and only, but the last and greatest of all the messengers of God conceived in this manner and born on earth.

This brings us to another point of consideration before presenting the ancient, mystical story of the birth of Jesus. In a previous chapter, I stated that the Essenes, the Nazarenes, and the mystics of Palestine, anticipated the coming of a great Master who would be the incarnation of one of the former great leaders. I also stated that it was the common belief among the Jews that the Messiah which they expected would likewise be the incarnation of one of their former deliverers. In these statements you will note the belief on the part of the people of the Orient in the *fact* of reincarnation, which was an established belief throughout the entire Oriental world and which is today a positive principle in the religious and philosophical thought of more than three-quarters of the earth's population, questioned only by part of the people in the Western world. The Orientals also knew, through previous experiences, that the great Avatars and messengers of God which came to them from time to time as the evolution of the races required, were the reincarnation of the previous great souls on earth, who had attained in each incarnation a higher and still higher degree of spiritual perfection and mastership. Just when each one of these messengers would appear in his *last and final incarnation* it was impossible for them to tell, but since all incarnations were progressive, and since each messenger was greater and more advanced than the preceding one, the Essenes, the

Nazarenes and even the Jews of Palestine, anticipated that the messenger who would come to them would be greater than any who had preceded him, and would probably be the incarnation of one of the greatest of those who had served them in the past. It was natural for the Jews to feel that such a messenger or Messiah would be the reincarnation of one of their previous deliverers, perhaps Moses, and most certainly of the House of David. On the other hand, the Essenes and those of the Aryan race believed (and based their belief upon a better understanding of the mystical laws than the Jews possessed) that the new great Master and redeemer for the world would be of the Aryan race, in the form of a reincarnation of one of the great Masters who had served the world in other lands and who would not be limited to the tribes of Israel.

For this reason, the Essenes in Palestine and in Egypt and other locations fully anticipated that from their own race and from among the members of their own organization would come the next great Master, because the Essenes represented at this time the group of most highly evolved and spiritually trained beings on earth.

CHAPTER V

THE MYSTICAL BIRTH OF JESUS

▽

EFORE giving the account of the birth of Jesus as it is recorded in the ancient Rosicrucian Records, I wish to call to the attention of my readers the following important points.

At the time of the birth of Jesus, the Essene Brotherhood as a part of the Great White Brotherhood was not only well-established in various parts of Egypt and Palestine with its largest center of members in Egypt, located at Alexandria, and its very large community district in Galilee, but the organization maintained a great secret temple at Heliopolis in Egypt where the Supreme officers met and where the highest ceremonies of the organization were held. This temple was often referred to in ancient records as the temple of Helios, or the "temple of the sun." In Palestine, a smaller temple for the sacred ceremonies of the Essenes in and around Jerusalem was located close to one of the Jerusalem gates. It was in this temple in Jerusalem that officers of the Essene Brotherhood in Palestine assembled for their high ceremonies.

Perhaps it is necessary to explain at this point, also, that in all the ancient temples of the Great White Brotherhood, including those of the Essenes, the young daughters of the highest members of the organization served as virgins or as *Vestals* for certain periods of their lives, and were under the guardianship of the organization. In all the Rosicrucian branches throughout the world today, including those in North America, there are several Vestals associated with each Temple or Lodge representing the spiritual consciousness of the Cosmic. These girls are always daughters of parents who have been in the organization for some time and are highly respected and aided in every way to high attainments in all the ethical, cultural, and educational principles of the land.

With these points in mind, I now present what is probably the oldest and most complete story of the Immaculate Conception and Divine Birth of the Master Jesus, as it has been recorded and preserved in the archives of the Rosicrucian organization in Egypt, India, and Tibet. I have had to condense the story slightly for presentation in this book, in order that the entire volume might not become too large, but I have not eliminated any essential detail nor altered any of the important mystical phrases.

The following story is one that is generally accepted with perfect understanding by the mystics of the Great White Brotherhood, and I trust that the mystics of the Western World will find in it a perfect explanation of this greatest of all mystical mysteries.

In the days of the mystic sects and sacred cults of the Great White Brotherhood of the Orient, there was one Joachim who was High Priest in the Holy Temple of Helios at the outer gates of Jerusalem. He was a devout follower of the sacred rituals and had pledged to give all that was his to the great work. And when the time came that his wife, Anna, was to have a child they agreed that if it should be a girl, and she should show *in her infancy* that she was divinely ordained, she should become a *dove* in the Holy Temple and remain a Virgin of the Sacred Sanctum. And in the ninth month Anna bore a child, and it was a girl as the astrologers (Magi) of the Temple, had predicted. When the days were accomplished, Anna purified herself, and gave the child the breast, and called its name *Mary* because the sun at birth was in the sign of Libra.

When the child was six months old it was taken by the parents to the Temple that the child might be examined and that which it carried from its last life revealed in the presence of the Priests and the Magi. The child was placed in the Sanctum upon its own feet, with its face toward the east, while the mother sat upon a white cloth at the foot of the Vestal Fire. The baby was urged to walk and it did walk. The Priests and Magi noticed that the child took *seven steps* and then knelt upon its knees before its mother in the Sanctum. And as the Magi chanted, the mother lifted up her child and cried aloud to the heavens: "As the Lord my God liveth, thou shalt not walk upon this earth until I give thee to the Temple of the Lord." And the priests glorified in the fulfillment of the prophecy that Joachim, their High Priest, should give to the Temple a virgin.

The mother was true to her promise. She made a sanctuary in her home and placed a cloth from the Temple of Helios upon the floor on which the child Mary should walk so that she set foot not upon the earth until the day of her deliverance to the Temple. The mother suffered nothing common or unclean to pass by her child and called the undefiled Virgins of the Priests of the Temples to lead her about the improvised Sanctuary and to carry her into the rose gardens when the sun was mellow.

The child's first birthday came and there was a sacred feast at the home of Joachim and Anna, and all the Priests and Scribes and Magi of the Temples of the Brotherhood were present. Joachim brought the child Mary from the sanctuary to the Priests, and she was sprinkled with undefiled water, and the petals of the rose, and the Magi proclaimed her officially named Mary, *the Dove of Helios.* The Priests blessed her and prayed to God, saying: "Oh, God of our Hearts, bless this child and make her name, as the Magi have just proclaimed it to be, a name to be eternally named in all generations of the sons of God." And all present said, "So be it, So be it, Amen!" Her mother then took the Dove to the Sanctuary to give it breast and she sang a song to God saying: "I sing thee a song, O holy child, a song unto God, for He hath given me the fruit of righteousness. Harken, ye Scribes of the Twelve Kingdoms of our land, for the Holy Dove is with me and God abideth with us." And when the feast was ended they went away rejoicing, each of the twelve Scribes to bring the great tidings to their Twelve Temples of the Twelve Kingdoms.

The months passed and the child became two years old and there was another birthday feast. And Joachim said, "Let us carry Mary to the Temple, that we may render the vow which we promised, lest perchance God refuse us the privilege and our gift become unaccepta' ble." But Anna, her mother, said: "Seest not that Mary is wise and strong for her years and blessed with an understanding not of this life but that which she carried with her to the mouth of my womb when she was born? In another year she will be stronger and of wisdom sufficient to permit her to journey to the Temple alone without her father and mother as in the past." And Joachim agreed. And when the child became three years of age and was exceedingly bright with inner under' standing, Joachim called the Priests and Scribes of the Twelve Kingdoms and invited the undefiled Virgins of the Priests to escort Mary to the Temple. The Virgins came with the sacred lamps burning with joy at the gift of God to the Temple. But Mary refused escort and was carried only by her Mother to the Temple gate, that her feet might not touch the earth. The Virgins were within the Temple chanting and incensing the Sanctum when Mary was received at the outer portal by the Priests of Helios. The child was then taken into the Temple and placed on the third step leading to the Altar while the Sacred Fire burned and the Priest prayed to God, saying: "God hath magnified his purposes and His name in all generations and through this child God will manifest His redemption to the children of this land." And he blessed the child and she danced with joy and walked from the Altar into the Sanctum and knelt before the Shekinah.

As the parents made their way toward the door of the Temple they turned and saw that the child asked not to go. And as the Virgins and Priests and the Scribes and Magi walked to the West of the Temple they cast rose leaves upon the kneeling child. The parents marveled at the child's desire to remain alone in the great Temple. When they had departed and the child was alone, Mary saw her own child body floating as a Dove in the air and from out of the space above the Shekinah there appeared a hand as though of an angel giving Mary *as she floated,* a morsel of food, and a voice, as if from the angel said: "Behold, this is to be thy food henceforth, for no longer shalt thou find milk at thy mother's breast, for thou hast sucked that which God hath provided and now thou shalt eat only that which thy kin shall serve thee."

At the time Mary became twelve years of age she was made womanly with functions which gave sign and symbol that her day had come to fulfill the vow of her parents. A council was held of the Priests and the Magi, who said: "Behold, Mary the Dove is become twelve years old and she giveth sign that her day either to dwell within the Temple or be given in marriage has come. Shall we take her now or wait the allotted time of twelve years and eleven months?" And the Magi replied: "Go before the Altar and ask God to show that which is right and whatever God shall manifest to thee, that also will we do." And Joachim, as High Priest, entered the Sanctum and placed upon his official garment the triangular breast plate, and prayed for illumination. And a form appeared to him, saying: "Joachim, Joachim, go forth and summon the widowers of the Brotherhood who hath homes and let them take a sacred staff apiece, and Mary shall be given to be cared for to him to whom God shall show a sign." And Joachim reported that which was given to him and the Scribes were informed to bring forth the widowers of their Kingdoms.

Now there was one, by name Joseph, who was of the Essene community at Galilee, and who was a devout Brother of the Temple of his Kingdom; and when he heard that all the widowers were summoned to Helios, he laid down his axe and tools with which he was build- ing a house, and hastened to meet the others. When all the widowers were assembled before the Temple of Helios, the High Priest selected 144 sacred staffs and purified them before the Altar and gave each of the widowers a staff. But there was no sign given by which Joachim could tell the answer to the selection the voice promised. Joseph was the last to receive a staff and as he lifted it in sacred salutation to the High Priest, be- hold a white dove went out of the rod and hovered over

THE MYSTICAL LIFE OF JESUS

the head of Joseph. And the High Priest said to Joseph:
"Thou has been alloted to receive the Virgin which
hath been given to Helios, to keep with thyself in thy
home." But Joseph refused, saying he knew not what
was intended by the gathering and that he had two
sons and he was old, and the Virgin appeared to be a
young girl not yet thirteen as was the law. The High
Priest admonished Joseph, reminding him what God did
to Dathan and Abiram, and Korah, how the earth
opened and they were swallowed up because of their
gainsaying. And Joseph feared, and offered to take the
Virgin and to keep with himself the Dove of Helios.
And he said to Mary: "Behold, I have received thee
from the Temple of God, and I will leave thee in my
house and go to finish my building and will come to
thee." And thusly came Mary to live with Joseph, the
widower and builder, as the Virgin of the Brotherhood.

And there came a time when the council of the priests
of Helios was called to make plans for the making of a
new curtain for the Temple. And the Priests said, let
us call the undefiled Virgins of our Brethren and also
our Dove of the Temple. And when the call was answered there were seven virgins. And Mary was sent
for as the Dove of the Temple. When they were within
the Temple, the High Priest ordered that lots should be
cast to see who should spin the gold for the curtain and
who should spin the green, the scarlet, the purple, the
blue, and the fine linen and silk. And the true purple

and scarlet fell to the lot of Mary, their Dove. And she took the materials and went away to her home.

As she worked upon her spinning there appeared to her a figure of a great Master who said: "Fear not! I come to bring thee a message of great joy, Mary, Holy Virgin and Sacred Dove of Helios, for thy day hath come to fulfill the prophecy of the Magi. Thou hath found favor with God and thy Brethren, and now thou shalt conceive from the *word* of God." And when Mary heard this she disputed, saying: "Shall I conceive from the *word* of God? And yet shall I bear as every woman beareth?" And the voice of the figure said: "Not in the manner of thy understanding shalt thou conceive, but in the manner of thy understanding shalt thou bear. For though the lips of man may kiss thee as the hands of the High Priest hath blessed thee, so shalt the seed of man be the heritage; but the *word* of God shall be breathed upon thee and its power shall make thee holy and bless the seed that it may be of God. Wherefore, also, that Holy life which shall be born of thee shall be called the Son of God, and he shall attain the name *Jesus* because he shall be the *God in Man* and will become the God with men." And Mary answered: "It shall be according to the *word* of God!"

Mary wrought the purple and the scarlet and took it to the High Priest. He spoke to Mary and told her he had been informed that her day had come to conceive and he blessed her and rejoiced with her, and told her that her name would be holy in all the generations of the earth. Mary went away, in time of preparation, to her cousin Elizabeth, and stayed there until her condition was so manifest that she again sought the privacy of her home sanctuary.

Her sixth month came and Joseph returned from his housebuilding and found Mary was with child and he was surprised and sorrowful. He smote his face and threw himself upon the sackcloth of the sanctuary and wept bitterly, saying: "With what face shall I look to my God? for I receive a Virgin, and the Dove of our Temple, and have not guarded over her and she has been defiled by man? Who hath done this thing in my home? Is not the history of Adam repeated in me?" And Joseph arose from his sackcloth and called Mary and said to her: "Why hast thou who walked the seven steps and was raised to the third step of the Holy of Holies in our Temple, permitted man to defile thee? Didst thou not receive food from the hands of an angel as a token that thou wast not to accept from the profane that which would feed thy earthly desires?" And she wept bitterly that Joseph did not know and that he should mistrust her, and she cried: "I am pure and know no man!" And Joseph was filled with awe and challenged her words, saying: "Whence then is it that thou art thus?" And she said with sweetness of voice: "As our God liveth I know not how this came but through the *word*! As I slept *He* came unto me with pureness of spirit, freed from the mortal body, and whereas **He** breathed not the breath of lust but spake with the breath the *word of God*, I conceived in fact as God first conceived in thought; and as the thought preceded the creation of the world, so with me the most holy of all words preceded the quickening that came upon me."

And Joseph was afraid lest those who knew not of the laws of God would misunderstand and misjudge, and he was in a quandary. But in the night there came to him the voice of the Master, saying: "Be not afraid, for that which she hath conceived is of the Holy Spirit, and she shall bear a son and the Heavenly Hosts shall call his name Jesus because the Holy Spirit, through the *word* of God, shall be in him."

And there came later, a Scribe to the home of Joseph to inquire about his absence from a meeting of the Brotherhood and the Scribe saw that Mary was with child and he went forthwith to the High Priest and was ready to *attest* that Mary had been defiled. And the High Priest sent for Joseph and Mary and gave them hearing and listened knowingly to Mary's declara' tion of innocence and purity and then reasoned with the Scribe. The Magi consulted and it was decided that the test should be given whereby their auras would mani' fest the color of sin, if sin there be upon them. And each was given a drink from the vessel containing the radiant water and they were placed in the dark and naught but pureness of Light came from them and no sin was made manifest. And the High Priest said: "If the God of our Temple manifests not thy sin through his laws, then I cannot judge you." And he dismissed them as pure in heart and clean in body.

The day came when Joseph found it necessary to journey with Mary to avoid censure because of his predicament and Mary's strange experience. And they came to a cave where they rested at Mary's request for she believed her hour at hand. Joseph sought aid and met a woman who came to the cave and met Mary and heard the strange story and believed it not. And in all directions Joseph saw that the heavens and the earth and the distant people upon it were silent and motionless and he knew that the presence of God was upon the face of the earth and that some miracle was about to be wrought. While he and the woman waited in the cave, a great Light came into the darkness and repelled them and it hovered over Mary. And the Light became smaller in size and more dense in white-ness until it enveloped Mary and then slowly reduced to naught. And as Joseph and the woman watched in the silence the Light was gone and there came the cry of a baby's voice and an angel appeared and said unto them: "At this hour, in humility of spirit, and with pureness of mind, to a Virgin in the Temple, there is now born the Son of God, conceived by the Holy Spirit through the *word* of God, and his name will become Jesus, for that it is name of God into which the fire of spirit and the power of the word is given. But I warn thee not to tell to the profane that which has happened, for they will believe thee not but will say that unto a Virgin some mortal man hath given child; and they will curse thee as a defiler of thy trust."

Joseph and Mary made ready to depart from the cave where they had been some time and were met by the Magi who came, saying: "Where is the great King whose star in the heavens declares his birth? This hour should see him and his parents upon the highway for his hour of birth is passed." And Joseph said: "I come unto Judea with the Son of God, not the King, for his Kingdom is not of the land but of the hearts of men."

And when Herod heard that a great King was born who fulfilled the strange predictions of the prophets, he made inquiries and was troubled. And when the Magi of the Brotherhood heard what Herod threatened, they warned Joseph, while blessing Mary and giving to her of their script, gold, frankincense, and myrrh. And Joseph and Mary proceeded on their way by another road.

CHAPTER VI

THE BIRTHPLACE AND THE MAGI

▽

IT MAY not be generally realized that there is a very interesting story in connection with the birthplace of the Holy Child, and for many centuries the exact *location* of the place has been an important point of discussion, and is even disputed at the present time among the highest authorities.

We note in the Christian Gospel of Matthew the inference that Jesus was born in a house in Bethlehem. The words of Matthew are:

"Now when Jesus was born in Bethlehem of Judea in the days of Herod the king, behold there came wise men from the East to Jerusalem, saying, 'Where is he that is born king of the Jews? For we have seen his star in the East, and are come to worship him . . .' And when they were come into the *house,* they saw the young child with Mary, his mother, and fell down and worshipped him."

No comments are made in the usual Christian Bible in regard to the Matthew statement that Mary and the child were in a *house,* and this difference of location usually passes unnoticed. We must bear in mind that the writer of the Book of St. Luke distinctly implies that the child was born in a *stable,* in the following words:

"And she brought forth her first-born son and wrapped Him in swaddling-clothes and laid Him in a manger; because there was no room for them in the inn."

Just why the almost universal impression exists that Jesus was born in a manger when there are two different statements in that regard will be explained in a moment. The fact of the matter is that in the early Christian days there was a third version of the place of birth that was exceedingly popular and based upon information not generally revealed in the present-day Christian stories.

We find, for instance, that Eusebius, the first ecclesiastical historian, who played an important part in the council of Nice, in 327 A. D., when most of the important traditions of the Christian church were discussed and decided, brought the matter of the birthplace of Jesus before the council for a positive decision, and in his discussions he said little about a house or a manger being the reputed birthplace of the holy child, but said that the youthful Jesus was born in a *cave* instead. And he referred to the fact that at the time of Constantine a magnificent temple had been erected on the site of the *cave*, so that Christians might worship the place where the Saviour was born. In the apocryphal gospel called *Protevangelion,* written by James, a brother of Jesus, we find reference to the *cave* again in the following words:

"But on a sudden the cloud became a great light in the cave, so their eyes could not bear it."

Of the prominent Fathers of the Holy Christian church in the early days, we find that Tertullian (A. D. 200), Jerome (A. D. 375), and others, said that Jesus was born in a *cave,* and all the heathens of Palestine point to the *cave* in their land to this very day as the birthplace of the Christian child.

We find also that Cannon Farrar said: "That the actual place of Christ's birth was a cave, is a very ancient tradition, and this cave used to be shown as the scene of the event, even so early as the time of Justin Martyr in A. D. 150."

Now the facts of the matter are that Matthew was nearly correct when he said that Jesus was born in a *house,* for the cave in which the child was born was more than an empty excavation under a rock, or a hollow place in the mountainside. The Rosicrucian records and the Essene records have always contained the statement that the child of Mary and Joseph was born in an *Essene grotto* on the highway near Bethlehem.

I have previously referred to the fact that the Essenes possessed certain rescue houses and hospices in various parts of Palestine, and three of these were grottos. Usually such grottos were partly natural and party artificial, and we know that grottos of this kind were quite common throughout Palestine and adjoining lands, for in the early Christian days it was found safer and better to build grottos than large structures above ground when the purpose of such places was protection, isolation, and safety. The number of grottos still existing in Palestine always surprises the investigating tourists, and many of them are large enough to contain from ten to twenty rooms of a fair size, free from moisture, dampness, heat, or cold.

The Essenes made their three grottos very large, very convenient in location, and well-protected from casual observation and attack by Bedouins or tribes-men. Such grottos were located from twenty to sixty feet below the earth's surface, with rooms that were approached by well-cut stone stairways descending at a wide angle and well-lighted by apertures in the side of the rock or rocks that protected the entrance way. Some of the rooms were carefully hewn out of solid rock while others were partly natural in their forma-tion. In most cases, the surface of the rock walls of the rooms was covered with a mud cement over which decorations or paint of some kind were applied in an artistic manner. Oil lamps, hung from the ceilings or set in niches in the walls, furnished ample illumination, and small apertures between the rooms, or rising up-ward into transversed channels, provided a proper cir-culation of air. Seats, or the foundations for lounges, were cut in the sides of some of the walls, or were formed of rocks in the center or end of the rooms. There was always a well close to each of these places, and provision was made in each room for a large jar of fresh water. The floor of these rooms was usually finished with partly smoothed stones, much like flag-ging, and only in one or two of the smaller rooms used for storage or some other purpose, was the floor left with its ground finish.

These grottos were usually furnished with convenient places for sleeping, eating, rest, recreation, and the care of the sick. In every way the appointments and equipment within these grottos were equal to those found in the mud, stone, or clay structures that were built above ground, and a *grotto home,* or hospice, was not considered less costly or less elegant than one that was built above the surface.

It was into the *Essene grotto* near Bethlehem that Joseph and Mary went for the birth of the child. A few references in the ancient Essene and Rosicrucian records regarding the event would indicate that it had been quite common for the women of the Essene organization to go to one of the Essene hospices for the delivery of their children, for a number of these places were prepared to take care of the sick, the injured, and the needy, as hospitals do, and it was traditional among the Essenes as it is today among the Jewish people, to give considerable thought and to provide unusual facilities for their women at the time of delivery. We might almost say that some of these early hospices were the originals for the present day *lying-in hospitals* so wellestablished in various parts of the world.

I recently visited this Essene grotto near Bethlehem, and carefully investigated the size, shape, and arrangement of the rooms, and I cannot see how any one of the millions of persons who have seen the birthplace of the Holy Child, can believe that there ever was any justification in calling it a *manger*. The large reception room in the center of the grotto, surrounded by many private rooms, immediately indicates that it was either a very large home, much larger than any home commonly found in Palestine, or a public place of some kind. The stone stairway descending to the rooms would certainly suggest that the place could not have been used as a stable, and when one sees the careful carving of the stones, the decorations still visible in many places, the care with which the floors were finished and the arrangement of the rooms leading off from the central room, one is impressed at once with the fact that this was undoubtedly a very well-planned and cared for hospice of some kind. Even today, the rooms are dry enough, warm enough, and comfortable enough for pleasant living, and when one sees the crude structures above ground that are *usually* provided for cattle (when any structures are provided at all) it is quite evident that no one would have gone to such trouble and expense for the sake of providing a stable for cattle.

At one of the famous Christian councils held by the early church fathers, when so many of the doctrines, teachings, and disputed points of tradition were being discussed and definitely settled, it was finally voted that the best way to end all of the argument about the birthplace of Jesus was to arbitrarily determine that a *manger* was the nature of the enclosure in which He was born. This arbitrary decision settled the matter for all time,

THE MYSTICAL LIFE OF JESUS

so far as the Holy Church was concerned, and regard-less of the many authentic records that still exist, it is probable that the story of the birth occurring in a *lowly manger* will remain a part of the Christian traditions.

One other important point in connection with the place of birth and the event of the birth of the Holy Child is likewise interesting. This pertains to the visit of the Magi and the homage they paid to the Holy Child. According to the authorized Christian versions the three *Magi* were led by a great star which caused them to journey "from the East" to the very locality in which the child was born. And they carried with them treasures and gifts of gold, frankincense, and myrrh.

The story of the star appearing in the heavens at this particular time has always been a fascinating one, and is also one that skeptics or doubters of the Christian traditions have looked upon as a fantastic element, in-troduced in the account merely to make it picturesque. But long ago scientific astronomers, who investigated this matter with their charts of the periodicity of famous comets and moving bodies like unto stars, dis-covered that *at* or *about* the time of the birth of the Holy Infant, there was a great star or heavenly body that was making its rapid movement across the heavens above these lands. Not only did this discovery, which has been substantiated by many scientists for many years, tend to verify the story of a symbol that could have led the *Magi* in their journey, but the many ancient traditions regarding similar stories reveal the fact that it was a common belief among the *Magi, the astrologers, the Chaldeans,* and the mystics of the Oriental countries, that whenever a great comet appeared in the sky and moved across the heavens, a leader or great *Avatar* was about to be born who would prove himself to be a Saviour or Redeemer. So well established was this belief, and so many interesting mystical points are involved in it, that I believe it worth while to take a little time at this point to speak of these matters.

It is true that in the story told in the Book of Luke, the writer says nothing about *Magi* from the "East," but he says that shepherds came and worshipped the young child, and that these shepherds had been keeping their flocks by night, and that the angel of the Lord appeared before them saying, "Behold, I bring you good tidings of great joy—for unto you is born this day in the city of David a Saviour, which is Christ the Lord."

That statement in the Book of Luke was evidently written for the purpose of trying to explain the ancient belief that when a great star appeared, moving across the heavens, it was a message from God that a Saviour was born, and the writer of Luke reduces the idea to a definite statement made by the Lord to the shepherds in the field.

In investigating the origin of this belief, we find from the old Essene and Rosicrucian records that when the Divine child called Chrishna was born, a great star in the heavens proclaimed the fact, and Chrishna was immediately adored and honored by the *Magi,* who brought gifts unto him. The old records state that the gifts consisted of *sandalwood and perfumes.*

At the time of the birth of Buddha, a great moving star in the heavens proclaimed his divinity, and the wise men again visited the place of birth and paid homage and presented gifts.

The birth of Confucius in 551 B. C. was heralded by a great star moving across the heavens which was observed by the wise men, who found the location of the great child through the movement of the star, and who went to the place of birth and paid homage. We find the same story in regard to Mithras, the Persian Saviour, Socrates, Aesculapius, Bacchus, Romulus, and a host of others.

We must remember that astrology was the one highly developed science among the *Magi* and mystics of the Oriental lands, and that out of this science grew the present-day science of astronomy. It may be inappropriate, but I cannot fail to take this opportunity of stating that the ancient practice or art of astrology was more highly developed than it is today and did not deal with the petty things of *luck* and *misfortune* with which our present-day astrology deals, and which so shamefully blasphemes an ancient and honorable mystical science.

The Magi referred to in the Bible were not just astrologers, or mediocre philosophers, who might have also been shepherds in the field, or ordinary persons of every day affairs, but were the learned instructors and high representatives of the great academies and mystery schools of the Orient. The title of *Magus* was granted only to one who had attained the very high degree of initiation in the mystery schools, and who had proved himself a master of the arts and sciences, and who was a highly evolved mystic in every sense. The *Magi* were consulted by the kings, potentates, and learned people of all lands, not only in regard to matters of astrology or astronomy, but in regard to history, medicine, natural law, spiritual law, and hundreds of other subjects which required profound thinking and unusual learning to ex' plain or comprehend. They were the great oracles for the learned. They even occupied the position of the highest advisers in courts and councils of last appeal in disputes of many kinds.

That a few of these *Magi* should have observed the symbolic star and noted its significance was but natural in their time. But we must not presume that their observance of the star occurred only a few hours before the birth of the Holy Child, and that they hurriedly left their sanctums or their places of occupation and journeyed rapidly across lands to the birthplace. Ac' cording to the ancient records at our disposal, we find that, as in all other cases, where the symbolic star had been noticed, the movement of this particular star had been observed for many months prior to the birth of the Holy Infant. For several weeks prior to the birth, close and careful tabulations had been made regarding the movement of the star, and the probable time of its ultimate significance. And those who had been selected by the mystery schools to journey to the place of birth and represent the Essene Brotherhood and the Great White Brotherhood had started on their way to Palestine several weeks prior to the time of the birth.

We find from the records, also, that these *Magi* knew the story of the selection of Mary as the preordained mother of the Holy Child, the location of the home of Mary and Joseph in Palestine, and the arrangements that Mary should go to the grotto hospice of the Brotherhood near Bethlehem for the delivery of her child. The record states that Mary was at the hospice three days before the child was born, awaiting the important hour. The *Magi* were in the vicinity of Bethlehem, also awaiting the hour. When the star appeared in the heavens at its highest point and then began its sudden and rapid descent toward the horizon, the *Magi* knew that the day and hour had come—and they had but to journey a short distance to the grotto to see the child that had been expected. They brought not only the things that are itemized in the Christian account, but greetings from the highest officials of the Great White Brotherhood, jewels of a symbolic nature for the mother and father, and a rosary containing a rare emblem for the Infant to wear about its neck, that it might ever after be identified as the anticipated *Son of God*.

The *Magi*, after having officially visited the child and formally presented their gifts and greetings, journeyed on to Mount Carmel and there made a report of the birth, and left official instructions for the keepers of the monastery and school at Carmel in regard to the educa' tion and care of the child throughout its infancy and childhood. Then these *Magi* went on to Egypt and made their report to the High Priests and the Supreme officers of the Brotherhood.

CHAPTER VII

THE BIRTH DATE OF THE HOLY CHILD

∇

THERE has always been considerable discussion regarding the year in which Jesus was born, and it is not my purpose to participate in this discussion at this time. The fact of the matter is that the actual year, according to the vari- ous calendars then existing and now existing, is of little consequence, for a definite year in one calendar would be a different year in another calendar. It would be very difficult for the average person to work out a calendar which would enable him to figure correctly the true year of birth. That the writers of the Books of the Bible were confused in regard to the actual year is very apparent after even a casual examination of their statements. For instance, in the Book of Matthew, we are informed that Jesus was born in the days of Herod, the king, and the writer of the Book of Luke states that Jesus was born when Cyrenius was governor of Syria or later. These two facts immediately offer opportunity for serious discussion, for Cyrenius was not governor of Syria until some ten years or more after the time of Herod. Even the matter of the taxing referred to in the stories indicates that a different year is referred to than is commonly accepted as the year of the birth of Jesus.

The very interesting point in regard to the time of birth, however, pertains to the *day* of the month and the month itself.

For many centuries after the life of Jesus, the Holy Fathers of the early Christian church, and the eminent ecclesiastical authorities were unable to decide as to the birth date of Jesus. Among the early Christians, the anniversary of the Nativity was celebrated with a great festival in May, sometimes in April, and on other occasions in January. Some of the earliest traditions in the Christian church definitely stated that the 20th of May was the correct date, while some of the Holy Fathers insisted that the 19th or 20th of April was the true and correct date. Even up until the fifth century after the life of Jesus, the matter was still in dispute, but in that century, the community at Rome held one of its famous Councils and made a definite decision and selected the 25th, or midnight of the 24th of December, as the true time. And in this decision we find a very beautiful and important *mystical story*.

It must be understood by my readers that the many facts revealed in this book which are different from the authorized Christian versions of the life of Jesus are not facts which were *concealed* during the early Christian days, but were *known to all of the Holy Fathers of the Christian church* and to the high ecclesiastical authorities who gathered in Councils from time to time and established the doctrines, traditions, and forms of ceremony to be officially a part of the Christian theology.

What motives these early authorities and Holy Fathers had for disregarding facts known to them, and for with' holding from the mass certain facts of intense interest to us at the present time, and in changing other facts to symbolical falsehoods, must be left to the intuition of my readers. The popular statement that "the end justifies the means" was unquestionably one of the thoughts in their minds. We find in the writings of these early authorities a statement made many times that certain changes and inventions which they estab' lished in connection with the traditions of the life of Jesus were "theological necessities." In other words, in order to utilize many of the ancient, mystical cere' monies, which the Holy Fathers derived from the temples of Egypt and from the doctrines and practices of the Essenes and the Great White Brotherhood, they had to *invent* certain points and principles in connec' tion with the life and work of Jesus, in order to make these ceremonies adaptable and consistent. In order to establish a new theology and many new doctrines, they had to ignore and set aside many facts which would have been inconsistent with their decisions.

When, however, it came to some important points that had to be definitely decided, they were forced to rely upon the ancient principles and doctrines that had been established, and were known to be *true spiritual laws* so that they would have some foundation upon which to base their decisions. The decision that *mid' night of the 24th of December* was the actual birth time of Jesus, was one such case, and the reason for this is intensely interesting from a mystical point of view. This decision, however, conflicted with one of the points in the traditional story of His birth, namely, the story that at the time of the birth *shepherds were in the field caring for their flocks.* It has always been said by those who knew the conditions in Palestine at that time that during the latter part of December is not a season when shepherds are in the fields caring for their flocks at night, or at any other hour of the day, and that this incident was introduced in the story when the belief was common that Jesus was born in the month of April or May.

However, the great fact which the Holy Fathers had to take into consideration in reaching their decision was that throughout all the centuries preceding, all the other great Avatars who had been born of Virgins, who were *Sons of God,* and who were known as Re- deemers or Saviours, had been born *on or about the 25th of December.* The other fact that they could not fail to consider was that there was a *spiritual law* or a *Cosmic law* for the birth of these great men on the 25th of December, and that no Redeemer of the world could have been born *at any other time.*

We must bear in mind that the birth of a great Avatar or a *Son of God* among men is not a *simple incident* in the scheme of things, nor a *casual accident of conditions.* The birth of an Avatar is the result of certain laws preordained and established in the Cosmic

THE MYSTICAL LIFE OF JESUS

scheme, and coincident with a series of events leading up to and culminating in the Divine Birth. The Cosmic birth of Jesus, as of every other Avatar, is an interest-ing story in itself, and has no place in this chapter, but in order that my reader may be familiar with the mani-festations of this great Cosmic law, I will present the following facts from the historical records of the Great White Brotherhood.

In the first place, there is a correspondence between the Spiritual law, Cosmic law, and Mundane law, per-taining to a universal condition manifesting about the 23rd, 24th, or 25th of each December. It is at this time that a Cosmic change occurs called the *Birth of God Sol,* and this event was always celebrated by the ancients as *The Accouchment of the Queen of Heaven* or the Celestial Virgin of the Sphere.

In India this period was one of great rejoicing every-where. Many centuries before the Christian Era, this period in December was celebrated as a religious festi-val, at which time the people decorated their homes with garlands and they were prolific in their gifts and presents to friends and relatives. So far back in an-tiquity can this religious festival in December be traced that its origin is lost in obscurity.

In China, also, long before the Christian period, the people recognized this period of the *winter solstice* as a holy time, and on December 24th, or 25th, they closed all their shops, their courts, and their places of business activities. Among the ancient Persians, their most splendid ceremonials were in honor of Mithras, whose birthday was recorded as having occurred on the 25th of December.

Among the ancient Egyptians for many centuries, the 25th of December was celebrated as the birthday of several of their gods. We find this referred to in all of the histories of the religions of ancient peoples, as, for instance, in the book entitled, "Religion of the Ancient Greeks," by De Stephenes, who says: "The ancient Egyptians fixed the pregnancy of Isis (the Queen of Heaven and the virgin mother of the Saviour Horus) on the last day of March and towards the end of December they placed the commemoration of her delivery."

In some cases the celebration of the birth dates of some of these ancient gods was changed by high proclamation, just as the birth date of Jesus was changed from May to December. The birth date celebration of Chrishna is now held in July or August.

In Bonwick's "Egyptian Belief" we find a verification of what is contained in the Rosicrucian records. He says in regard to Horus: "He is the great god—loved of Heaven. His birth was one of the greatest mysteries of the Egyptian religion. Pictures representing it appeared on the walls of temples. One passed through the holy *adytum* to the still more sacred quarters of the temple known as the birthplace of Horus. He was presumably the child of deity. At Christmas time, or that answering to our festival, his image was brought out of that sanctuary with peculiar ceremonies, as the image of the infant *Bambino* is still brought out and exhibited in Rome."

It is interesting to note here that the word "Bam' bino" is now a sacred word among the foreign Chris' tians, and is a term used for representations of the infant Christ Jesus in swaddling clothes. It is customary in Rome to bring out to public view early on Christmas morning, an image of the *Bambino* carried with great ceremony for the public to salute and greet, in honor of the original birthday. This little incident of Roman Christian ceremony is just a continuation of the ancient customs established in the mystic lands by the Great White Brotherhood.

Osiris, son of the holy virgin, or *Neith,* was born on the 25th of December; and the Greeks celebrated this day as the birthday of Hercules.

Bacchus and Adonis were also born on the 25th of December. Tertullian, Jerome, and other Fathers of the early Christian Church who labored so diligently in the formation of Christian doctrines, ceremonies, and creeds, inform us in their early writings that the ceremony of the celebration of the birthday of Adonis on the 25th of December, took place in a *cave* and that the cave in which they celebrated this mystery was in Bethlehem, and was, in fact, the *same cave* in which the child Jesus was born. This is but another verification of the fact that the *Essene grotto* in which the Holy Child of Mary and Joseph was born had been used for the celebration

The Christian figure of the *Bambino*, or the Christ child. It is this form carved in marble or stone that is exposed in the churches on Christmas morning and kept on view from Christmas to Epiphany. It is claimed that Saint Francis of Assisi was the originator of this statue in the thirteenth century, but research has revealed that a similar statue of a Holy Child was exhibited on Christmas Day in many lands before the Christian Era.

of previous Avatars, such as Adonis. This is why the *Magi* knew where to find the new Avatar on His birthday.

The fact that the 25th of December was celebrated generally as a day associated with the birth of *Sol,* or the Cosmic birthday of certain laws and principles manifested by the Sun, is shown in many ancient records of the early Christian celebration in Rome. We can turn to the writings of the Rev. Gross, who has written very thoroughly and authentically in regard to these matters, and read as follows: "In Rome, before the time of Christ, a festival was observed on the 25th of December, under the name of *Natalis Solis Invicti* (birthday of Sol, the Invincible). It was a day of universal rejoicing illustrated by illuminations and public games. All public business was suspended, declarations of war and criminal executions were postponed, friends made presents to one another, and the slaves were indulged with great liberties."

It is interesting to note, also, that among the ancient Germans centuries before the birth of Christ, these people celebrated annually, at the time of the *winter solstice,* an ancient, sacred period which they called their *Yule-feast.* On this occasion all agreements were renewed, the gods were consulted as to the future, sacrifices were made to the various gods, and the people indulged in jovial hospitality. Of this ancient ceremony the word *Yule* still survives as the old name for Christmas, and the ancient custom of burning the *Yule* log

on Christmas Eve is still the usual practice. It is interesting to note also that the word *Yule* in French is
called *Noel*, which is the equivalent of the Hebrew or
Chaldee word *Nule*. Among the ancient Scandinavians
there was a yearly celebration at the *winter solstice*
that was observed as the *mother-night*, and the feast was
called *Jul*. It was in honor of *Freyr*, the Holy Son of
the supreme god and goddess. The celebration included
all sorts of demonstrations of joy and happiness, and the
bestowing of gifts.

In Great Britain and Ireland the Druids celebrated
the 25th of December as a holy day, and burned great
fires and lights on the tops of hills. Even in ancient
Mexico, the last week of December was celebrated as
a sacred feast, in honor of the birth of a god.

The use of evergreens and mistletoe at Christmas
time derived from ancient practices, and Tertullian, the
Holy Father to whom I have referred previously, writing from a distant land to his holy brethren at home,
described this custom of December 25th and the use of
evergreens and mistletoe, and said that it was "rank
idolatry." He went on to describe how they decked
their doors "with garlands of flowers and evergreens."

From the foregoing we see that when the Great
White Brotherhood in Egypt set down in its records
the statement that *the day and hour of the winter
solstice* was the Cosmic period for the births of Avatars,
as observed in all the ancient notations, it was not
ordaining a time or arbitrarily establishing by decree a

period for the celebration of the birthdays, but was merely proclaiming *what it had observed* and proceeded to state how the Cosmic law had made itself manifest. Just why Avatars should be born in the *winter solstice* and why so many of the great leaders of men were actually born at such a time, is a matter that deals with the principles of reincarnation, Cosmic cycles of existence, and Cosmic laws, relative to the periodicity of the stages of advancing civilization. Such points as these have no place in the present volume.

Of course, those who are interested in the profound mystical principles and spiritual laws of the universe, and who are anxious to know just how these affect every man and woman in his or her personal development and attunement with the Cosmic Consciousness, will make contact with some school or system which deals with these subjects thoroughly, conscientiously, and without bias or prejudice. Naturally such information is never sold and never put into book form for public sale at any price. For this reason the seekers will vainly search among book stores or in the offerings of private publishers or commercial movements for the information desired. Only such organizations as the Rosicrucians, for instance, or branches of the Great White Brotherhood operating in foreign lands, will give the seeker this information without price in a private, personal way, and with no other motive than the benefit that each individual will derive from the instruction, if he or she is found worthy to have such knowledge.

CHAPTER VIII

THE BOYHOOD OF JESUS

▽

E FIND two periods in the authorized Christian version of the life of Jesus which are passed over without comment and without detail. These are the years constituting His childhood and up to and including His appearance before the learned men in the Synagogue, and the period from that time until the beginning of His mission in the Holy Land as an adult.

The silence in Christian literature regarding these two periods has unquestionably been responsible for a great many discussions that have led to severe criticism of the entire story of His life. Aside from the orthodox version of His birth, which so many reject because they do not understand it, the two gaps in the story of His life referred to above have constituted excellent reasons for the rejection of the story of the remainder of His life. Those who cannot accept the Immaculate Con- ception and Divine Birth of Jesus do not hesitate to point out the two gaps in the early part of His life as proof that the real story of the life of Jesus has never been told.

The highest critics of the authorized version of the life of Jesus point out with some justification that if the Biblical accounts did not go into such detail and put such great stress upon the events of His conception and birth, the absence of details regarding His childhood and youth would be immaterial, and would cast no reflection upon the entire story of the latter part of His life. But when every important and casual event leading up to His birth, and the events of the birth itself, are recorded by so many witnesses, and glorified in such detail, there appears to be some significance in the silence regarding His youth. Surely those who felt it their duty to gather, record, and preserve the essential and non-essential points regarding the birth, and all that led up to it, must have had access to the facts pertaining to His childhood, and these facts must have been more definitely recorded and better known to a large number of persons than the events pertaining to the conception and birth of Jesus. Why, then, the silence and the complete absence of those details which would have been highly interesting and extremely illuminating to those who would adore the man and seek to worship every phase of His life?

Be it known, therefore, that the facts regarding the childhood and youth of Jesus are not lacking and are not absent in those records which were kept and are still preserved by those groups of persons and organizations which have not been influenced by the rulings of religious councils or the dictates of synods and who do not find in those facts any event or any incident belittling to the greatness and supreme mastership of Jesus the Christ.

I am aware that some of the facts pertaining to the childhood and youth of Jesus have become public in various lands at various times and that some of these facts have found their way into the mystical writings of the occidental world. But the complete story and the most important details have been withheld by those organizations who know them well in the belief that until the Western world was ready to understand them in their richness and illuminating significance, it would be better to withhold them. There is no reason why these facts should not be revealed at this time, and I am glad to say that the authorities who have the records in their archives and with whom I have recently held consultation in this regard, agree that the present rest-lessness throughout the Western world in regard to religious matters, and especially the desire on the part of so many millions of persons for a more complete out-line of the life of Jesus, warrants the publication of the facts now given for the first time in Western sacred literature.

That Jesus must have had some unusual preparation and very thorough education is quite apparent to any student of Christian doctrines, and to every analyist of the life of this great man. The mere fact that at an early age He could astound the learned men of His country by His ability to answer and ask profound questions, proves that during the first ten or more years of His life, He was carefully educated and carefully trained. We may assume with perfect reason and logic that as a Son of God or a messenger of God, He was inspired continuously, and could find in His immediate contact with the Consciousness of God the illuminating thoughts which He expressed. But with the same reasonable logic, we must believe that He had to receive that education and training in the mundane schools of this world, which would make it possible for Him to *express* those ideas and those thoughts in the words and tongue, in the images and pictures, understood by the multitude.

The greatest of the masters in art have undoubtedly painted their masterpieces under inspiration. Nevertheless, each of these masters had to be trained in the technique of expressing that inspiration in a medium that would convey the thought, the idea, the picture, from one mind to another. The greatest of the composers have unquestionably written under inspiration, and by their own admission found that the most beautiful passages in their music came to them as from Heaven; nevertheless, these men had to be trained in the technique of expressing that which was inspired within their souls.

No matter how completely and perfectly Jesus may have been in spiritual contact with the Cosmic Mind and with the Consciousness of God, He had to have that training, that education, and that practice in the use of words and in the expression of thought which enabled Him to say the most beautiful things in the most beautiful language ever spoken by man. We cannot conceive of an uneducated, untrained, unprepared instrument speaking such thoughts and doing such things as He did, even under the most perfect inspirational contact, without preparation and training.

The argument that any such training and preparation in mundane schools and at the hands of earthly advisers, instructors, and guardians would weaken the claim of Divine preparation and unique Sonship, is absolutely absurd. Have we any reason to believe that the mother of Jesus did not teach the little child to walk, or to eat? Or shall we assume that these things were Divinely inspired in Him, and that from the moment of birth such things were known to Him? After all, is not the matter of walking upright, instead of crawling about, a matter of earthly wisdom and regulation, and not a rule of the Cosmic or an establishment of God, which God would inspire in the minds or consciousness of all beings? Is not the use of certain words, of certain languages, and the grouping of these words into grammatical phrases, a result of man's regulations and rules rather than Cosmic laws and principles? If these things are earthly products, then they must be acquired at the hands of men on earth, and must be taught by men.

Most certainly Jesus was taught to speak the Hebrew, the Aramaic, and the Greek languages, for we cannot conceive God having inspired the knowledge of these languages in the consciousness of Jesus without earthly education; for why should these three languages have been selected by God as the modes of expression on the part of one who was to be a Redeemer of all peoples in all lands, with many tongues? If Jesus was taught how to speak, and taught several languages, and the ability to interpret the inspiration of His soul into sounds and words that would convey a meaning to man, there is no reason to believe that He was not taught other things necessary to carry out His great mission in life. All this is for the purpose of presenting the logic and reason- ableness of His education, and not for the purpose of attempting to prove that He must have had such educa- tion. There are ample records to show *how* and *where* He was educated, and these we will deal with at this time.

In the first place, I have already shown that Jesus was born in the family of two devout Essenes and in a community of Essenes. This in itself was sufficient to guarantee the young child the very highest education obtainable in any land at that time. Not only were the preparatory schools conducted by the Essenes sufficient to give every child an excellent education at the hands of teachers and masters who had been trained in many lands and raised to the highest degree of ethical and literary attainments, but the associations and connec- tions which the Essenes maintained with their other branches in foreign lands guaranteed a very liberal edu- cation to this special Son of God, and this special charge of the Essene Brotherhood.

We are told in the accounts of His birth how the Magi, who were the learned wise men of the mystery temples and the chief instructors of the highest principles of education, came to the birthplace of Jesus to pay homage to Him, as the preordained Avatar of the new cycle. This acknowledgement on the part of the great Magi indicates that the little child was anticipated and expected by the Brotherhood and by the Great White Lodge in all lands, and would be guided and protected throughout His life. To assume that these Magi paid such homage and adoration to one whom they knew to be the great and expected leader of humanity, and then never showed any further interest in His education, development, and training, and played no part in the development of His life, is to assume something that would be more of a mystery than any other phase of the life of Jesus as it appears in the authorized Christian version.

I have said that at the time of the Birth of Jesus, the Essenes constituted a large community in Galilee, and that they had hospices and refuge houses in various parts of Palestine for the care of the poor and needy. They also maintained the Supreme Temple in distant Egypt and minor temples in Palestine and other places. I must point out now one other fact that has been held in secrecy for many centuries, and which will probably explain many strange references in the sacred literature of the Christians and other sects.

The Nazarenes, the Nazarites, and the Essenes had united their interests in regard to one essential work, and it was this that is referred to by many authorities in religious and sacred histories and encyclopedias as being one of the common interests which bound the Nazarenes, the Nazarites, and the Essenes. This work was the maintenance of a great school, college, and monastery on Mount Carmel. The introduction of this historical place into the life of Jesus may seem surprising to a great many of my readers, and for this reason a brief resumé of the history of Mount Carmel may be not only appropriate, but of value to those who wish to make further research in this regard.

Just when the Mount of Carmel became the secret, sacred place for the maintenance of an isolated, protected school of mystics, and of the Great White Brotherhood, is not definitely known. The earliest historical incidents of a religious nature connected with Mount Carmel are those associated with the lives of Elijah and his son. The ancient Jewish documents, as well as many of the writings preserved by the Roman Catholic Church, which in later years became greatly interested in the Mount of Carmel, show that from the earliest period of the history of this Mount, there was located there a tabernacle, monastery, or temple of some kind, and that when Elijah went to this mountain to carry out the many marvelous things recorded of him, he found a temple and an altar there. We also know, from references in various records, that many of the great masters of the Great White Brotherhood spent part of their lives on this mountain in the temple or monastery. Even Pythagoras spent part of his life there, and in the history of his life this retreat of Mount Car- mel is referred to as "sacred above all mountains and forbidden of access to the vulgar." We find even in the Roman Catholic records, which have traced the history of Mount Carmel very carefully, references to the fact that "in ancient times the sacredness of Carmel seems to have been known to other nations besides Israel, thus in the list of places conquered by the Egyptian King, Thothmes the Third, there is a probable reference at Number 48 to the 'Holy Headland' of Carmel." Those who are students of Rosicrucian history know that Thothmes the Third was one of the great founders of the early mystery schools of Egypt, and a leader in the movement that became the Great White Brotherhood. The Rosicrucian records also point out that Thothmes the Third in the year 1449 B. C., conquered Carmel and released it to those who sought to maintain in this out-of-the-way place a school and monastery for the mystery teachings.

Now it is well known that Elijah was a Nazarite and an Essene, and that both the Jewish and Roman Catho- lic records refer to him as such. This one fact alone would be sufficient to indicate the nature of the demon- strations which Elijah performed on Mount Carmel and the nature of the monastery and temple maintained on the summit of the mountain.

In many of the old stichometrical lists and writings
and papers of the ancient ecclesiastical writers, mention
appeared of an apocryphal "Apocalypse of Elias," from
which some citations are said to be found in Corinthians
(1) 2:9, and elsewhere in the Bible. This old book or
Apocalypse of Elias was known to the mystics of the
Great White Brotherhood and is known to all of the
Oriental Rosicrucians as a very sacred record of the
early history and teachings of the Essenes and the Nazarenes. In the early Christian centuries and during the
lifetime of the Master Jesus, the Apocalypse of Elias
was well-known and used in the sacred classes of the
most advanced members of the organization. But like
many other very valuable and illuminating records of
early periods dealing with the more secret teachings, it
was withdrawn from public use and became "lost."
However, in 1893, Maspero, the famous historical
writer connected with the Rosicrucian Order of Egypt,
found a Coptic translation of it in one of the Brotherhood's monasteries in Upper Egypt. Since then several
other translations in other languages have been discovered in the archives of the Great White Brotherhood, and parts of these have been used in the recently
issued higher teachings of the Rosicrucians. From this
Apocalypse of Elias and from the other Rosicrucian
records, we learn much about the establishment of the
monasteries and schools at Carmel, which were known
as "the school of the prophets" or "the school of the
Essenes."

As years passed by, the attendance at the school and monastery at Carmel became so large that a community was established there, composed of those who were students, and they adopted a distinct form of dress and remained within the monastery grounds throughout their entire lives except for the periods that they went forth to other lands as missionaries. It was here that many of the most ancient manuscripts were translated and illuminated on parchment and sent to the various archives of the Great White Brotherhood throughout the world. A wonderful library was also maintained at Carmel for many centuries. Members of this community were present at Saint Peter's first sermon on Pentecost, and they built a chapel in honor of this occasion. Many other historical structures existed there, such as El-Khadr, the school of the prophets, El-Muhraka, the traditional spot of Elias' sacrifice, Elias' Grotto, and the monastery itself.

About four hundred years after the Christian period, the monastery and school at Mount Carmel were abandoned as the principal place of education for the Great White Brotherhood, and the wonderful library and the thousands of manuscripts and records were transferred to the secret monastery of Tibet, where these things are now preserved, and where the greatest school of mysticism and sacred literature in the world is maintained. Some centuries after this abandonment, an Order of a monkish nature was established in Carmel, and the members of this organization claimed to be descendants of those of the original organization, but likewise claimed to be Roman Catholic in faith. This contention caused much dispute for several centuries and was finally settled when Pope Innocent XII in 1698 decided that the claim of direct succession was not cor-rect, and that the new organization had no connection with the early Carmelite Brotherhood. Out of this de-cision grew the present organization known as the Carmelites, or White Friars, as they are called in Eng-land, which is a Roman Catholic organization popular-ly known as the Carmelite Order. Today in the midst of the ruins of the ancient Essene structure can be seen the Roman Catholic convent of the Carmelite or-ganization.

According to the Rosicrucian records, we find that in the sixth year of His life, the youthful Jesus was placed in the school at Carmel and began his prepara-tion and training as a Son of God and an Avatar. There is no question about the authenticity of this statement. It is recorded in too many places and in too many different ways, and verified by so many later incidents in His life, that any question of this fact cannot be reasonably raised. The records further intimate that while He was an apt and perhaps unusually bright stu-dent, He was given every special advantage that the entire organization, not only in Palestine, but in Egypt as well, could give to one that was known to be their special charge and the greatest among them. It is also recorded that young Jesus was not entered in the school under the name of Jesus, but under the name of Joseph, and this presents another interesting fact for those who desire the most intimate details of His life.

It is commonly believed by Biblical students that the name of Jesus was given to the child at the time of His circumcision, in accordance with the custom of the land. This is based upon the fact that He was called Jesus later in His life, and that before His birth it was said that His name would be or should be Jesus. The Gospel of St. Luke tells us the familiar story of how an angel appeared to Mary and told her that the unborn child would be called Jesus. But this statement and that in St. Matthew are really prophecies. They say simply that Mary *shall* bring forth a child who *shall* be known as Jesus. In the historical record presented in Chapter V of this book, we find that Mary was told that the "holy life which shall be born to thee, shall be called the Son of God, and He shall *attain* the name of Jesus."

Nowhere in the Christian Bible do we find the state' ment that He should be christened Jesus at the time of the circumcision, but we do find reference to such naming at His circumcision in the Gospel of the Infancy of Jesus. But these statements were added to these Gospels on the presumption that the name He bore later in life was the name that was given to Him at circum' cision. The Gospels were written long after the lifetime of Jesus, and contained similar assumptions and infer' ences without foundation. From the time that the dis' ciples knew Jesus or came in contact with Him, until the close of His life, He was known as Jesus and bore that name. Since they never knew him or contacted Him before He bore that name, they had no reason to believe that He ever had any other name. The fact that such a name was predicated for Him and that He eventually attained such a name, causes us to investigate the meaning of the name *Jesus*.

We know that the word "Christ" comes from the Greek word "Christos" which means "Messiah." We find that the word "Christos" was introduced to other nations when the Septuagint was prepared about 100 B. C., and that it was used to translate the word Mashiach which means "the anointed one," or, in its more complete form, Meschiach, meaning "Jahveh's Anointed." The word or title "Christos" had been used in the mystery schools and in the Orient for the name and title of many of the former Avatars. Even Cyrus is called "Christos," and in the Psalms CV:15, the plural form "Christis" is used to apply to the patriarchs. In the Old Testament, the word "Christos" is limited to mean a Jewish King, except in the case of Cyrus and the patriarchs, which exceptions prove that it could mean a man *great* in *more ways than one*.

Going back to the Septuagint, we find that the Greek word "Christos" originally came from the name of one of the Egyptian deities. There was old Hermes, whose name has been corrupted or translated into "Haram of Tyre," who built the temple without the noise of axe or hammer. The Latin form of this name is Mercury, while the Greek form is Hermes, and the Egyptian form was Tachut. Now in Hebrew, the word "Tachut," which is called "Thoth" occasionally in Greek, means "under" and "beneath." Thoth was the Lord or God of Maa, or the Egyptian Maa or Maat, meaning "truth." And Maa kHeru, meaning "true words" is the basis from which came the Greek form "Merkury" or "Mercury."

The Egyptian letter or dipthong "kH" is a highly aspirated H and by the Greeks is usually transcribed as X and, vice versa, the value of the Greek X is usually transcribed as "ch." The kHeru of the Egyptians would be therefore, "cheru" or "Ch-R." These latter letters form the famous "XP," or the cryptogram of the early Christians, which I personally saw and traced on several stones of the tombs in the Catacombs of Rome. It is generally accepted in all Christian historical records that this "XP" referred to Christ, and in the Greek Gospel of John, Jesus is called the *Logos,* which is a word having a similar meaning. Therefore, we see that the term "Christ" was a title to be specifically applied to and attained by one who had been especially born and deified as a messenger of God.

Now the word "Jesus" presents the same under-standing. The old Hebrew form of the word is found in the Old Testament of Joshua, or Jeshua, and was often rendered as Jesu. The Greek form of the name is responsible for the final s. Originally, the Hebrew form of Jeshua means "helped of Yahveh," while the later

THE MYSTICAL LIFE OF JESUS

Hebrew form means "to deliver" or "to save." There-fore, Jesus came to be known as meaning "saviour."

In the Synoptic Gospels we do not find the disciples at first calling their master by the name of Jesus, but they did call him "Rabbi" meaning "teacher" and "Adthonai" meaning "master," and other titles of respect and love.

The record of His entrance into the school at Carmel shows that He was entered as Joseph, the son of Mary and Joseph, and the reincarnation of *Zoroaster,* the "Son of God." When and how He attained the name of *Jesus* is explained in another part of this work.

CHAPTER IX

JESUS ENTERS THE PRIESTHOOD
▽

HE ONE definite comment made on the early life of Jesus in the popular stories of His life, especially those of churchly origin, tells about the wonderful impression which the child made upon the learned Doctors and Masters at the time of His visit to Jerusalem in His thirteenth year. Even among the most advanced of Christian theologians and in nearly all of the extensive histories of His life, the real facts pertaining to this visit to Jerusalem are misunderstood or misrepresented through a lack of knowledge of what actually occurred.

I have already said that Jesus and His parents lived as Gentiles in the Gentile section of Palestine but had to obey the Jewish customs and regulations of the land. One of these regulations was that in accordance with strict Jewish law, it devolved upon each boy in his thirteenth year to attend one of the feasts at Jerusalem. He had to appear officially under certain conditions and at a certain place for a definite ceremony, and then become what was called "a Son of the Commandment," or "of the Torah." The usual time for such a visit was on the first Paschal Feast after the boy had passed his twelfth birthday. According to the story, the parents of Jesus took Him with their other children in the company of other Nazarenes to Jerusalem. The text of the Christian version seems to indicate that it was "their wont to go" up to the temple. This is evidently a mistake on the part of the writers or translators, because as Gentiles, the parents of Jesus were not accustomed to attending all of the feasts and ceremonies of the Jewish church, for the law did not require that of any but those who were strictly orthodox and wholeheartedly affiliated with the Jewish religion. Since Jesus was the first born of the children in the family and, therefore, the oldest, He was the only one of the children of Mary and Joseph who had attained the age when such visits were compulsory, and so this must have been their first obedience to this law of the land. I find that even some of the highest critics of Christian literature agree that the phrase "it was their wont" to go, should be read in that sense which puts the participle to the present tense and not in the aorist. Hence we understand how glad Mary and Joseph were to avail themselves of this opportunity to visit the Holy Sanctuary in Jerusalem, and bring their wonderful child before those officials who would conduct a formal examination.

This Paschal Feast in Jerusalem was held in the spring and Caponius was acting as Procurator, and Annas ruled in the temple as High Priest. Out of Galilee walked this holy family, accompanied by a host of other Gentiles, Nazarenes, Nazarites, Essenes, and some Jews, chanting as they went, and making of the event a gala occasion. The ranks of these travelers swelled by other festive bands who united in chanting the *Psalms of Ascent* to the accompaniment of the flute, and unquestionably discussing the spiritual principles involved in the ceremonies to be held. It was a long journey as we would view it in these days. Recently I made the trip in a very fast automobile from Nazareth to Jerusalem, and found that it required the better part of a day to do it. All through the beautiful section of Palestine which these pilgrims had to traverse, composed of hills and valleys, magnificently tinted with the beautiful green of that country and spotted with flowers, one could still see the ancient trail of foot-paths that led up over the hills and down into the valleys in almost a straight line from the present site called Nazareth to Jerusalem and over which the pilgrims walked in their journeys to and fro. Even today the natives of that country walk these same paths or ride on their donkeys garbed as in the times of Christ, presenting a picture that carries one back hundreds of years.

When the tired pilgrims finally reached the gates of Jerusalem, the problem of being housed and cared for must have been a serious matter, for the Feast brought nearly the entire population of Palestine into the environs of Jerusalem for three or four days. The Essenes, Nazarites, and Nazarenes were fortunate inasmuch as at the city gate, and in places nearby, there were special houses and structures owned by the Essenes and Nazarenes for the care of their own people and for pilgrims and strangers who needed their care.

The scene must have been a glorious one for the youthful child, making perhaps the first long trip in His life. The school at Carmel is but a short distance from the village of Galilee, as compared with the long distance that stretches between them and Jerusalem, and we may easily realize how impressed the child must have been with the sight of so many pilgrims, the chanting, the music of the flute, the wayside prayers, the excitement, and finally the greeting and preparations at the city gate.

So little has been told about the Temple and Sanctuary where Jesus attended the Feast that perhaps a few words about this place will be of interest to my readers. As the pilgrims reached the place of the Temple, they found it necessary to ascend a mount crested by beautiful buildings symmetrically proportioned and gigantic enough to hold within its walls not fewer than two hundred thousand persons. The mount on which the structures stood rose abruptly from out of the valley, much like an island that rises out of the sea. And around it, in the greenness of the valley, was a mass of walls, palaces, houses, and streets reflecting the bright sunlight from the snowy marble and glittering gold. About one thousand square feet of the mount was occupied by the Sanctuary and Temple. At the northwestern angle and connected with the main structure was the Castle of Antonia held by the Roman garrison. The lofty walls were pierced by massive gates. One unused gate known as the Tedi was on the north;

on the east was the Susa gate which opened on the arched roadway to the Mount of Olives. There were also the two Huldah gates, which led by tunnels from the priest-suburb *Ophel* into the outer court, and on the west were four other gates.

Within the gates the court was surrounded by double colonnades with benches here and there for those who resorted to prayer, or for conferences. The southern double colonnades, with a wide space between, were the most magnificent. The eastern colonnade was the most venerable, and was known as the ancient "Solomon's Porch." Entering the court from the bridge under the tower of John, the pilgrim would pass along the southern colonnade to the eastern extremity over which rose a tower known as the *Pinnacle*, and referred to in the history of the Temptation. From this lofty pinnacle, the priests each morning watched and announced the sunrise, and four hundred and fifty feet beneath this tower yawned the Kedron valley. Within these colonnaded areas were the meeting places of the first and lowest of the three Sanhedrins, known as the Temple; and the second or intermediate court of appeal usually held in what was called the Court of the Priests; and the highest of the courts known as the Great Sanhedrin, which was often referred to as the "hall of hewn square stones."

Passing out of the colonnades and porches, one would enter the court of the Gentiles, or what the Jews called the Mount of the House, which was the widest on the west side. This was called the *chol*, or profane place to which the Gentiles retired during the Feast, and it was here also that the market place was located for the sale of various needful articles, along with the money chang' ers. Beyond this Gentile section was a wall which marked a space beyond which no Gentile or no person not strictly orthodox might proceed. Thus, the Gen' tiles, which included the Essenes, Nazarites, the Naza' renes, and those who had not adopted the Jewish faith completely, had to assemble in a special place set aside for them.

The Sanctuary itself was on a higher terrace than the Court of the Priests. Twelve steps led up to its porch, and here in separate chambers all that was neces' sary for the sacrificial services was kept. A two-leaved gate opened into the Sanctuary which was divided into two parts. The holy place had the golden candlesticks in the south, and the table of the Shewbread in the north, with the golden altar of incense between them. The mystical *Veil referred* to so often in the ceremonies of the mystery temples of Egypt, from which the Veil in the Jewish sanctuary was derived, concealed the entrance to the most Holy'Place, which was an empty place in the temple containing nothing but the *piece of rock,* the *Ebhen Shethiyah,* or foundation stone, which, according to tradition, covered the mouth of the pit, and on which the world was founded.

These few details cannot give an adequate idea of the vastness of the temple buildings, for all around the sanctuary and colonnaded courts were various chambers and outbuildings which served different purposes connected with the services.

It was in the Gentile section of the entire enclosure that Joseph and His parents along with the others of their class assembled. It was necessary for the Gentiles to be present only for the first two days of the Feast. On the third day, therefore, were held the special ceremonies for the strictly orthodox, and for the rest of those in attendance, the third and following days were so-called "half-holy days" when it was lawful for all in attendance to return home if need be. It was at this time that Joseph was brought before the learned doctors immediately after the ceremony for examination and questioning. Undoubtedly there were many other children of His age present on this occasion, and undoubtedly the questioning was the same for all of them, but we are told that the answer which Joseph gave provoked intense interest in Him, and that after the usual questions had been asked of all the children, and the parents and children had proceeded on their way, young Joseph was retained for further questioning and a special examination.

We are told in old records that it was customary on the last days of the Feast, and when the actual Feast itself had been celebrated and the usual ceremonies completed, for the doctors of the Temple-Sanhedrin to come out upon the terrace of the Temple and there to preach or discuss certain doctrines and conduct a forum, or ask questions of those in whom they were especially in-terested. It was in such an audience as this, out on the terrace and informally conducted, that Joseph was found after His parents had started on their way home with their other children and missed Him, according to the Christian version of the story.

As I have intimated, there was nothing extraordinary about the fact that one or more children had been re-tained by the doctors for special examination. Many writers of the life of Jesus, and many Christian authori-ties who have analyzed this incident in His life, have attempted to speculate upon the nature of the questions and answers which brought Jesus to the attention of these doctors. Some of them seem to have come to the conclusion that Jesus was taking part in one of the usual scientific classes designated as *Kallah,* at which time not only the doctors but the most analytical of the Jewish scholars discussed the doctrines, practices, cus-toms, and habits of the Jewish church. Such sessions required considerable preparation on the part of the lecturing Rabbis or doctors, and considerable Talmudic knowledge on the part of the attendants.

Many of these discussions dealt with the establish-ment of new rules and regulations, and the authorita-tive interpretation of Jewish rules. For instance, the great Hillel took part in a discussion in this court re-garding the propriety of offering the Passover on the Sabbath, and by his great logic proved that it was ap-propriate to do so, and was honored for his services in this regard. It is hardly to be believed that the youthful Joseph could or would participate in such discussions as were common to the *Kallah,* even if the learned doctors had considered Him old enough or wise enough to be present. Furthermore, the fact that Joseph was a Gentile, and not of the strictly orthodox faith would have prevented Him from participating in this class. And there is another consideration: these classes were held in the last month of summer (Elul) before the feast of the new year, and in the last winter month (Adar) immediately before the feast of the Passover, but it was in the spring that Joseph attended the Paschal Feast.

Another speculation on the part of some theological writers is to the effect that perhaps the parents of Joseph, realizing that the boy was about to enter into a new cycle of His life, informed Him regarding His Divine Birth and Sonship and that He in turn presented these facts to the learned doctors at the temple and discussed the important principles involved. This explanation is more unsound than any other, for the simple reason that the young man was on His way to the temple in obedience to a law which definitely outlined the procedure and the purpose of the occasion, and it would have availed Him nothing to have argued in behalf of His special appointment from on high. It is very doubtful, indeed, if the doctors assembled at the court would have permitted Him to make any plea or explanation in behalf of His own Divine place in life, and certainly would not have set aside other tasks to listen to any such unique presentation.

We can thoroughly understand just what did happen when we examine the facts in the case, and re-enact the entire scene. The youths of Palestine were called upon to come to the temple in their thirteenth year in order to partake of the Paschal Feast, and thereby aknowledge obedience to the Jewish religious law. It was a purely formal *registration* intended to supply the church with a complete list of those who had attained that age where they could be counted as of the faith or out of it. It was natural, therefore, that before being permitted to partake of the Feast, every young man was questioned in a categorical manner, being asked a list of questions, which would reveal the religious faith and ideas of each applicant. These questions had been asked for many years, and considered a standard catechism. The cate-chism for Gentiles was different from that used for those who were strictly orthodox, and born in the faith. In other words, the questions asked of those who were assembled in the Gentile section of the court were quite different from those asked of the youths assembled in the orthodox section.

Our records indicate that Joseph had been somewhat prepared by His education at Carmel and by His con-tact with the orthodox Jews to answer the questions that would be asked of a Gentile registrant at the Feast. It was their belief that only such questions would be asked of Him as were asked of other youths, and that

He would answer them in proper manner, that made the parents leave their child alone in the class for youths while they went into an adjoining building where adult Gentiles were given a different examination, prepara- tory to participating formally in the Paschal Feast. It was probably the plan that after young Joseph had finished His examination and had entered the Sanctu- ary along with the other youths in the Gentile class, He would meet His parents out in the general court and proceed with them on their return.

According to the story, the parents proceeded home- ward with their other children, and with a large band of others who were returning to Galilee, and it was not until they were half-way home that they discovered that young Joseph was not in the large party of pilgrims. The fact that His absence was not noticed during the first part of the trip plainly indicates that young Joseph was relied upon to take care of Himself and to look after His own interests, and that the parents were more concerned with the care of the younger members of the family.

That young Joseph was well-educated, unusually alert of mind, and in every sense well-prepared to take care of Himself is not only indicated by this incident but by what actually happened in Jerusalem. It is recorded that during the formal examination, and while young Joseph was answering the categorical questions put to all of the youths, He gave explanations in regard to some doctrinal points that involved a new angle, a broader insight, and a higher idealism regarding the mystical side of the theological points than any of the children being examined. This so surprised the learned doctors that they asked young Joseph to remain after the class had completed its work, and after they had all partaken of the Paschal Feast. He was then called before a group of the learned men of the Great Sanhedrin and further questioned, and then requested to remain within the temple grounds until the following day, when He would be interviewed by a court composed of the highest officials, High Priests, and learned teachers. It was here that young Joseph was found on the third day.

According to the records, I find that young Joseph did not put any particular emphasis upon His Divine appointment as a *Messenger of God,* nor refer in any particular manner to the preordained mission of His life. He did reveal the fact that He was a special student of the Essenes at Mount Carmel, and that it was His intention to carry out the plans of the Brotherhood and visit the higher schools of instruction in foreign lands, including the academy and mystery school at Heliopolis. What this may have indicated to the minds of the learned Jewish doctors is not definitely stated. One question put to young Joseph does indicate that they immediately suspected Him of being a *selected leader* for the future work of His Brotherhood. However, this in itself would not have aroused any curiosity or particular interest on the part of these doctors, and evident ly it did not antagonize them, inasmuch as they did not express any idea regarding young Joseph's apparent refusal to do otherwise than accept merely the *formal commandment* making Him an *adopted Jew of the country.*

Their surprise and keen interest centered around the unusual insight that young Joseph had regarding re-ligious, theological, and mystical principles, and His very clear exposition of spiritual laws. For this reason they were amazed at His "combinative insight" or un-usual spiritual intelligence and "discerning answers." If young Joseph had revealed to these doctors some of the principles taught by the Essenes, and was the apt student which the Brotherhood records in its reports, then He must have astounded these doctors who were learned only in the traditional teachings of their own faith, and unaccustomed to the newer and higher ideas taught in the Brotherhood schools.

Young Joseph did reveal, however, in very positive terms, that in a few months He would finish the pre-liminary courses of instruction at the school at Carmel, and that in accordance with the rules and regulations of the organization, He would leave Galilee early in the fall to go to the schools in foreign lands, and that He would not return to Palestine for many years. Thus He explained His reasons for not doing more than formally obeying the command to appear for registration, and not promising to attend the Synagogues, regularly, or become a true disciple of the Jewish faith. The fact that He had been circumcised made Him *potentially* a Jew so far as fundamental preparation for admission into the Jewish faith as a Gentile was concerned, and there was no way by which the Jewish church could force this young man, or any other of the Gentile youths, to become an orthodox follower of the Jewish religion.

Young Joseph was not the first ambitious youth of the country who had gone to Egypt and other lands to acquire a higher education or to make more successful contacts with the larger things in life, and the fact of His determination to travel for the betterment of His education did not cause any surprise in the minds of these doctors. However, His entire attitude and the free and easy manner in which He spoke of His plans did surprise these men who were accustomed to having the youths of the land show them greater consideration and less independence.

So when the parents of young Joseph found Him sitting in the midst of a group of learned men, and succeeded in calling Him aside and reminding Him, He may have made the reply which Christian literature has made very famous, and which our records do not reveal at all. But if He did say that He had been very busy attending to His Father's business, we can understand that He was referring to the entire scheme of His life. Certainly He must have felt that He was about His Father's business when He was making plain to His inquisitors the nature of His beliefs and convictions, the reason for His contemplated journeys to other lands, and His inability to become a devout attendant at the Synagogues in Palestine.

After young Joseph and His parents returned to their home village, He was sent again to the school of Mount Carmel, there to live and finish His term of preliminary instruction.

CHAPTER X
JESUS ENTERS THE SECRET PRIESTHOOD

▽

ITTLE is intimated in the Christian Gospels about the life of Jesus between the time of His appearance before the learned doctors in Jerusalem and the beginning of His mission in Palestine. In fact, the first revelation regarding the preparation of Jesus for His work as a Son of God is in connection with His Baptism at the river Jordan. We are told that at this time Jesus came out of Galilee and permitted Himself to be known to the public.

Certainly the Baptism of Jesus could not have been the beginning of His preparation for the ministry; and most certainly more preparation than this was required to carry on the work which He efficiently conducted for so many years.

I have intimated in previous parts of this book why it is unreasonable to believe that Jesus required no preparation for His ministry, and I have tried to show that His whole life demonstrated deep study, careful preparation, and unusual guidance during His youth.

We now approach a period in His life that is not only interesting because it is generally *unknown* to the students of Christian doctrines, but is highly significant in the sight of the work which He accomplished during His lifetime.

According to the Essene records, young Joseph completed His official schooling early in the fall, when He
was still in His thirteenth year. With all of His pre-
cociousness and brilliant mind, He was not permitted
to shorten the usual period of study and preparation
in the School of the Prophets at Carmel. Therefore,
we must presume that He was given careful attention
and tutored by those who added such special subjects
to His instructions as would have kept Him engaged
in His attainment of knowledge until the prescribed
time had come for His transfer to other teachers and
other schools.

The records also outline very clearly and definitely
the incidents of His life from the time of the transfer
from Carmel until He was ready for His great mission.
The details of these incidents in His life are too exhaustive and unimportant to present *in toto* in a book of
this size and character, but the essential points and the
interesting incidents may be outlined as follows:

According to the instructions sent to the school at
Carmel from the Supreme Temple at Heliopolis, the
young Avatar was to complete His education by a
thorough study of the ancient religions and teachings
of the various sects and creeds most influential in the
development of civilization. In other words, He was to
become familiar with the tenets of the so-called *heathen
religions* before taking up the study of the development
of the pagan beliefs and rites into the higher principles
and creeds taught in the mystery schools of Egypt.

In modern times, the student in preparing for the ministry must become familiar with comparative religions, but he is able to do this in one great university, where the sacred books and writings of the ancient religions are expounded, analyzed, and carefully digested before the modern forms of theology are undertaken; he does not have to leave his own land and journey into distant places in order to contact and become acquainted with the ancient religions or schools of ethics.

In the time of which I am writing, however, it was considered absolutely necessary for the student of religion or philosophy to journey to the very seat of each of the ancient religions, where he might have access to copies of the authentic versions of each religion and an opportunity to live among the peoples, and become intimately acquainted with the rituals, rites, and practices of the tenets. Many of the great Avatars in the past had journeyed to distant places for this purpose, and it was in this way that knowledge of the various ancient teachings had become universally disseminated.

So young Joseph was placed in the charge of two *Magi*, who came to Carmel for the purpose of conducting the youth to His first distant school and place of experience. The records show that Joseph was permitted to spend about a week with His parents in Galilee, while the *Magi* made their preparations and held various consultations with the officials at the Carmel school. They also instructed the parents of Joseph as to what they should *expect* and what they should *do* in His absence. The records further state that when Joseph and the Magi started from Galilee, a special ceremony of the Essenes was held in one of their small assembly places, and that without attracting unnecessary attention, the Magi and the boy proceeded with a number of others who were going a short distance of the way, in caravan form, by the shortest route to Jagannath. This city was located on the east coast of India, and its present day name is Puri. It had been the center of pure Buddhism for many centuries; and on a mountain near the outlying districts of the town there was a monastery or school containing many of the ancient Buddhist writings and the most learned instructors of Buddha's doctrines. It required nearly a year for the Magi, young Joseph, and others, who joined the caravan en route, to reach this point in India, while the Magi continued to instruct Joseph. During their many trials and tribulations they pointed out to Him the sufferings of humanity, the weaknesses and strength of the people's ideals, and the popular fallacies of the day.

According to the records, young Joseph remained a little over a year in this monastery school, and became thoroughly familiar with the ancient teachings and the evolved rituals of the Buddhist faith. The principal teacher of young Joseph at this time was one known as Lamaas, to whom young Joseph took such a great liking that later in His life He sent for Lamaas to come and unite with the Essene Brotherhood in Palestine.

When it came time for young Joseph to leave the monastery at Jagannath, visits were made to the valley of the Ganges with a several months' stop at Benares. We must bear in mind that the great monastery and world hearquarters of the Great White Brotherhood had not yet been established at a spot in Tibet; for if it had been Joseph and His *Magi* would have undoubtedly proceeded to this place and remained there for a con-siderable time. In Benares, young Joseph had an oppor-tunity to pursue the study of ethics, natural law, language, and similar subjects constituting the offerings of several of the great schools there which were re-nowned for their culture and learning. It was while here that young Joseph became greatly interested in the Hindu method of healing, and took a short course in the Hindu principles under Udraka, who was reputed to be the greatest of the Hindu healers.

After a visit to other parts of India, merely for the purpose of contacting the art, law, and culture of the peoples, Joseph returned again to the monastery at Jagannath, where He remained for two more years. His advancement in the subjects being taught was such that He was appointed a teacher in a small town called *Katak*, and this gave Him His first opportunity to be-come familiar with the art of teaching or instructing by the use of parables or stories.

As a result of His contact with eminent teachers and learned men in Benares, young Joseph was visited by a high priest from Lahore. It appears from the records that He had already introduced new ideas and truly mystical principles in His discourses and instructions to children, and these appealed to the most learned of His hearers, but aroused the antagonism of the unlearned and strictly orthodox Hindus. Therefore, early in His life He learned what it meant to have enemies as well as followers. The high priest from Lahore tried to per- suade young Joseph to change His teachings slightly and at the same time cease His journeys among the lower castes and common people. Here was Joseph's first temptation to hold Himself aloof from the common touch and to change His attitude so as to appeal to the aristocracy and the influential. However, young Joseph refused to listen to the petitions of the high priests, and even refused to accept gifts that were offered.

It was while He was thus drinking the bitter draughts of life, that Joseph received the sad news that His father in Galilee had passed on, and that His mother was griev- ing, and none were able to comfort her. Messengers informed Him that no word had come from Him, and that His mother was unable to learn of His wereabouts; and even though informed by the Essenes that silence on the part of young Joseph had been predicted, and that He was safe, she could not be consoled. It was at this time that young Joseph expressed Himself for the first time in definite words, which were recorded and are still preserved. According to the several transla- tions of the message which He sent by the Essene mes- sengers to His mother, it read as follows: "Beloved mother: Be not grieved, for all is well for father as with you. He has completed his present work here on earth, and has done so nobly. None in any walk of life can charge him with deceit, dishonesty, nor wrong intention. In his period of life here he has completed many great tasks and is gone from our midst truly prepared to solve the problems that await him in the future. Our God, the Father of all of us, is with him now as He was with him heretofore; but even now the Heavenly Hosts guard his footsteps and protect him on his way. Therefore, why should you weep and suffer? Tears will not conquer your grief, and your sorrow cannot be vanquished by any emotion of your heart or mind. Let your soul be busy in meditation and contact with him who is gone, and if thou art not idle, there will be no time for grief. When grief throbs through the heart, and anguish causes you pain, permit yourself to rise to higher planes and indulge in the ministry of love. Your ministry has always been that of love, and in the Brotherhood thou canst find many opportunities to answer the call of the world for more love. Therefore, let the past remain the past. Rise above the cares of earthly things and give your life to those who still live with us here on earth. When your life is done, you will find it again in the morning sun, or even in the evening dew, as in the song of birds, the perfume of the flowers, and the mystic lights of the stars at night. For it will not be long before your prob-lems and toils here on earth will be solved also, and when all is counted and arranged, you will be ready for greater fields of effort and prepared to solve the greater problems of the soul. Try, then, to be content until I come to you soon and bring to you richer gifts than any that you have ever seen, and greater than those made of gold or precious stones. I am sure that my brothers will care for you and supply your needs, and I am always with you in mind and spirit. Your son, Joseph."

This letter and other writings, written during the years which followed and which have been carefully preserved and recorded, plainly indicate the rapid development of His mind, and the marvelous comprehension He had of Cosmic laws and principles.

It is stated in some ancient records that after Joseph had completed the studies of the Buddhistic teachings and the Hindu doctrines in India, He journeyed to Lassa in Tibet. While still in India, a messenger came to Joseph with some manuscripts from a Buddhist Temple in Lassa, sent by Mengste, who was considered the greatest of all the Buddhist sages. For a considerable period messengers from Lassa brought manuscripts to young Joseph, and it was this intercourse and the effects it had upon His life that may have caused Him to journey to Lassa, personally. However, when Joseph was ready to leave Jagannath, His journey took Him westward toward Persia, where, in the city of Persepolis, arrangements had been made for His further studies. This was one of the ancient cities of the kings, and the center of the learned Magi of that country who were known as Hor, Lun, and Mer. One of these *Magi*, a very old man, was one of the three who had visited the infant at the time of His birth in the Essene Grotto, and had brought to Him gifts from the monastery of Persia.

Great homage was paid to Joseph by these *Magi*, and by the priests of the temple. Other wise men from various sections of Persia came to Persepolis, and remained there as instructors and students during the time of Joseph's education; for it is recorded that at the close of each day when the instructors had finished the day's lesson, they asked Joseph to become their teacher, and inform them of the higher principles which He seemed to comprehend through inspiration.

It was here that Joseph finally made plain to the elders that the greatest instruction He had to give was that which He had obtained in the silence after meditating upon some important law given to Him in the course of His reading and studying. Thus, Joseph established a system of *Entering the Silence* which became an important feature in later mystical methods. It was in this city, also, that Joseph demonstrated considerable healing power, and after months of analysis of the power within His being, and a careful study of the principles involved, He revealed to His elders His belief that the faith of *mental attitude and attunement* on the part of the patients had a considerable effect upon the results. This laid the foundation for the later teachings of the secret conclaves of the Disciples of Jesus—*inner or psychic attunement and mental prep-*

arations are necessary in all forms of spiritual healing.

After a year spent in Persia, Joseph and His guides proceeded to the Euphrates. Here He contacted the greatest sages of Assyria, and Magi from other lands who came to see Him and hear Him speak; for He had already attracted great attention as an interpreter of the spiritual laws in a more understandable, mystical manner. Joseph spent a considerable time in the cities and towns of Chaldea, and in the lands between the Tigris and the Euphrates. His healing powers and methods were becoming so rapidy perfected that it is recorded that multitudes were benefited by His meth' ods in these lands; and it was about this time that the *Magi* who were His guides informed Him that the development of the ability to heal would be one of the tests in His final examination of preparedness for His ultimate mission.

From this country Joseph and the guides journeyed through the ruined Babylon, and spent some time in examining the fallen temples, ruined gates, and the empty palaces. It was here that He became familiar with the trials and tribulations of the early tribes of Israel when they were held in captivity in Babylon, and He saw where Daniel and the Hebrew children had their great tests. He was unquestionably impressed with the sins of pagans and the error of ancient beliefs.

Then Joseph and His guides journeyed to Greece, where He came in contact with some of the Athenian philosophers and was under the personal direction and

THE MYSTICAL LIFE OF JESUS

care of Apollo, who opened up the ancient records of Grecian lore for Joseph. In this country Joseph attracted unusual attention among the wise and the Magi, and they implored Him to remain a long time; but His itinerary had been definitely decided upon, and in a few months He sailed from Grecian shores for Alexandria.

He stayed but a short time at Alexandria, just long enough to be entertained by the special messengers who went there to greet Him, and to visit some of the ancient shrines. He was taken immediately, thereafter, to the city of Heliopolis and settled in a private home, arranged for Him, having several man servants, a beautiful garden, and a personal attendant whose records as a scribe would place him today in the category of a personal secretary.

Very shortly after His arrival in Heliopolis, Jesus was approached by representatives of the pagan priesthood of Egypt, who had heard of His teachings and His demonstrations of mystical power and disapproved of them. Once again He learned to drink of the bitters of life through many trials and tribulations which would have tempted the average person to accede to the advice of the priesthood and resort to hypocrisy and deceit in regard to His purposes and intentions.

It was at this point in His life that Joseph began His preparatory initiations for the entrance into the higher grades of the Great White Brotherhood, and I will treat these in my next chapter, for the details are worthy of complete presentation.

Chapter XI
JESUS ATTAINS MASTERSHIP
▽

IN ORDER to understand the advancement of Jesus through the various grades of the priest-hood leading to mastership, it is necessary to explain the operation of the Great White Brotherhood in which He became an initiate. The Great White Brotherhood referred to so often in the preceding chapters was a non-sectarian organiza-tion formed in a primitive way by the ancestors of Amenhotep IV, Pharaoh of Egypt, who became better known in philosophical literature as Akhnaton. We are not sure in regard to which of these ancestors was the first to proclaim the foundation of the Brotherhood, but we do know that Thothmes III established many of the important rules and regulations for the conduct of the Brotherhood, and that these regulations were in effect for many centuries. In one of the Rosicrucian records, we find that at the close of his reign as Pharaoh of Egypt in 1447 B. C., there were thirty-nine men and women constituting the high council of the secret Brotherhood. The council meetings were held in one of the halls of the temple at Karnak in Luxor where Thothmes III had erected two obelisks on which were carved the famous cartouche which became the seal of the Brotherhood and which is used in Egypt and America today as the seal of the organization known as the Rosicrucian Order. In establishing this cartouche as the seal of the organization, we find the following words written in the record in regard to its use: "In testimony of the great work of our teacher (Master) to be forever a mark of honor and loyalty."

The son and grandson of Thothmes III sponsored the continuation of the secret Brotherhood, and permitted it to increase in size and activity. In 1378 B. C., was born Amenhotep IV, the great grandson of Thothmes III, and he became the great reorganizer and founder of the present rules and regulations of the world-wide organization known as the Great White Brotherhood established in ancient times.

The original plan of the secret Brotherhood was to bring the wisest men and women in Egypt together, and especially the most advanced of the Magi, for the purpose of discussing, analyzing, recording, and preserving the great knowledge that constituted the light of the world. Egypt had become the center of the world's culture and scientific knowledge, as is attested by the remarkable attainments made by her people under the leadership of the wise men in the sciences generally. To Egypt went students from all parts of the world, to obtain the highest education and to contact the mystery schools, as they were called, under the direction of this secret Brotherhood.

Amenhotep IV was the reincarnation of one of the previous great Avatars and became what historians call the world's first great citizen. He, too, had a great message for the world, and during his short lifetime accomplished more for the advancement of philosophy, religion, and ethics than any man preceding him. It was he who began a very strenuous attack upon the heathen priesthoods of Egypt which held the masses in slavery, and it was he who established the world's first monotheistic religion, for Amenhotep declared that there were not many gods, but only One, "the ever living, sole God." In his doctrines, which he introduced into the Great White Brotherhood, he laid the foundation for the present-day monotheism and for most of the doctrines and creeds used in the Christian and Hebrew religions.

It was while Amenhotep was Pharaoh that the children of Israel dwelt in Egypt and the leaders of those tribes became initiates of the Great White Brotherhood, and it was at this time that Moses, as one of the initiates, became acquainted with the fundamentals of the religion which he afterward modified to present to those who followed him out of Egypt into Palestine. It was also to Amenhoptep IV that Moses made his appeal for aid in taking the tribes of Israel out of Egypt, and it was through the aid thus given by Amenhotep and by the Great White Brotherhood in secrecy that the tribes of Israel evaded the heathen priesthood and had a safe journey.

As stated in an earlier part of this book, branches of the Great White Brotherhood were established under various names in many parts of the world during the first ten centuries before Christ. The original body of members in Egypt became the international council or supreme body maintaining the name of the Great White Brotherhood and eventually adopting the rose cross emblem as their esoteric symbol. But the branches established in various parts of the world were per' mitted to adopt such names as were significant in the various languages, or symbolical to the peoples with which they had to deal. Thus it was that a large branch formed at Heliopolis adopted the name of the Essenes, which name was later used by the followers in the northern part of Palestine; whereas in Greece the name of "Therapeuti" was used, and other names in other places. All these branches, however, used the same seals and symbols, adhered to the same general rules and regulations, and paid allegiance to the supreme body known as the Great White Brotherhood in Egypt.

Out of the monasteries, schools, and temples of the Great White Brotherhood, and its branches, came most of the famous philosophers, teachers, priests, and Ava' tars of the future, and today we find that in the branches of the organization known as the Rosicrucian Order, which name has become practically the exclusive worldly name for the organization, there are students in preparation for the ministry, for positions as teach' ers and professors in colleges, those who are to become eminent physicians in various schools of therapeutics, including medicine and surgery, and those who are also preparing for research work in the various fields of science. In the membership, we also find the hundreds of thousands of men and women who are students of the teachings of the Rosicrucian Order, because of the personal benefit they derive, and the assistance the or ganization gives them through private teachings and instruction for the betterment of their living, the attain ment of personal evolution, and the awakening of those latent or dormant faculties which enable them to achieve the highest degree of success and happiness in their individual careers.

Therefore, it was natural that the new Avatar should be one of this organization, as had been most of the Avatars in preceding centuries. It was also perfectly logical and reasonable for this young *Son of God* to have His footsteps directed toward the great schools and teachers of the Brotherhood in Egypt, where He might complete His preparations and receive His final instructions before entering upon His divine mission.

Before any initiate of the Great White Brother hood could go out into the world and proclaim the doctrines and teachings which would enlighten civiliza tion and bring about the gradual evolution of humanity, he had to be tested and tried in such ways as would not only prove to the entire organization his worthiness to be their high representative, but would make him familiar with the tests and trials that would inevitably face him during his mission.

Thus we find Joseph now at the threshold of His final preparation and ready for the symbolical tests and initiations leading to the degree and attainment of mastership which would qualify Him to go out into the world and fulfill the mission for which He had been Cosmically and Divinely ordained.

The story of the Great White Brotherhood and its activities and achievements is more completely outlined in another volume entitled, "Rosicrucian Questions and Answers, with Complete History of the Order," and in this history the story of the attainment of mastership by other Avatars of lesser prominence is told. We are now concerned only with the attainment of mastership by the greatest of all these Avatars.

When Jesus was ready for His entrance into the supreme college and monastery of the Brotherhood at Heliopolis, He found that the first requirement called for three months of meditation, prayer, and study in the quiet of His own home, during which time many of the eminent masters of the Brotherhood would contact Him in the Cosmic or psychic sense, through mental processes.

The records show that He was surrounded, as we have stated, with every comfort and convenience, and that for His study He was given many of the rarest manuscripts containing the texts of ancient doctrines and creeds. Then came the first of the tests. It is stated that one night at the midnight hour, a door in His chamber was opened, and a priest in Oriental garb came to Joseph and pleaded with Him that He abandon His intention of staying in Egypt and receiving the authority of the Great White Brotherhood, because His mission and plans were antagonistic to the priest-hood of Egypt, and the priesthood was plotting to take His life, or to imprison Him. The priest offered various methods whereby Joseph might secretly and easily leave Egypt and return safely to Palestine. Young Joseph had seen many evidences of the enmity which His presence in Egypt had aroused, and as I have said be-fore, He was drinking of the bitter cup. For this reason the pleading and offering of the priest were certainly tempting. But young Joseph absolutely refused to abandon His plans or to change His decision. Joseph summed up His argument with the statement that "I shall not bargain with deceit, nor sell my soul for the safety of my body. I shall deceive no one, and I will be no partner of hypocrisy. Return to your people, and tell them that I shall remain true to God and to myself."

His decision was reported to the high authorities of the Brotherhood, and Joseph was commanded to ap-pear before them. Then the Hierophant placed his hand on Joseph's head and gave Him a scroll on which was written just one word, "Sincerity." Joseph knew that this had been a test of His sincerity and that He had yielded not to temptation.

Some weeks later another messenger called upon Joseph in His home, and presented a very interesting story. This messenger claimed that he had at one time been in the same position as Joseph, and had suffered all the trials and enmity of the priesthood of Egypt while he remained steadfast in his determination to be come a master. He claimed that he had attained high degrees in the organization, and had finally been admitted to their great ceremonies and to their secret conclaves, and that then he had found that all of the work was corruption, and that their rites were sacrificial, in which innocent children, women, men, and animals were burned as offerings to false gods, and that he had finally escaped and now urged Joseph to think well of the future and to stop before it was too late. When Joseph questioned him as to how he had gained access to His chamber, the man replied that as a trusted priest of the Brotherhood he knew of passageways and doors which permitted him to enter any of the structures of the organization. Joseph then accused the man of being a traitor and said that He would refuse to listen to one whose hands were not clean, and who could not show a higher purpose than he had shown. The man disappeared, and again Joseph was brought before the Hierophant who once more placed his hand upon His head and handed a scroll to Him which contained but one word, "Justice." And Joseph learned that this was another test and that He had passed it successfully.

About a month later, another priest approached Him one afternoon, when He was in the midst of meditation in the quietness of His sanctum. This priest began to comment on the grandeur and richness of the rooms in which Joseph dwelt, and he called the attention of Joseph to the fact that the great Brotherhood in Egypt had undoubtedly provided these luxurious surroundings for Joseph because to them Joseph was the greatest of them all, and that the healing Joseph had accomplished in foreign lands, the wonderful interpretation He had given in answers to questions asked in India and Persia had proved that He was the greatest philosopher, the greatest mystic, and the greatest teacher in all the world.

Therefore, he urged that Joseph should not submit to the dictates of the Brotherhood, but go out into the world at once and organize a priesthood of His own which would overthrow all others, and bring trium- phant victory to Him personally. It is recorded that this man made eloquent pleas to young Joseph and pointed out to Him the rosy path to fame and popular acclaim, bringing to Him wealth, honor, and unlimited power. The man left the presence of Joseph at the psychological moment of his beautiful presentation, and for many days Joseph wrestled with the idea that had been implanted in His mind, but always there came from within the voice of the Divine Self pointing out clearly the duty for which He had been Cosmically ordained. Finally Joseph sent a message to the man and stated that He was thankful for the contest that had raged within Him and for the victory which had come to the better self, and that He wanted not glory, fame, or wealth, but only an opportunity to serve and to keep the faith while life was in His body.

And once again He was called before the Hierophant, and this time a scroll was handed to Him upon which was written the one word, "Faith." And Joseph learned that this was another test of His faith and that He had passed it successfully.

Thus Joseph completed the first of the three preliminary degrees of initiation, which were really degrees of test and trial, before being admitted into the important Fourth Degree of the Brotherhood. Having passed these tests, and further examinations which were held before the conclave of High Priests, He was finally honored with the title of *Master* and admitted into the highest circle as a duly prepared and qualified *Master of the Great White Brotherhood*. This title of *Master* was always used by the Essenes in speaking of Jesus throughout His entire ministry, when the conversations dealt with His public affairs or the reference was made in general conversation aside from any of His special activities as a *Divine Son of God*. The title of *Master* was also used by many of the Jews who greatly admired Jesus for His work among them, and especially for the valuable instructions which He gave; and it was always reverently used by those who understood its real meaning, just as it is reverently used by the Rosicrucians today when they speak of the *Great Master Jesus*.

▽   ▽   ▽

CHAPTER XII

JESUS ATTAINS CHRISTHOOD

▽

AVING attained the degree of Mastership in the Great White Brotherhood placed Joseph among the most learned of the High Priests and second only to the Hierophant of the organization. This entitled Him to attend the highest conclaves, to have access to the most sacred and sublime ceremonies, to indulge in the transcendental experiences at certain Cosmic periods of the year, and to attune Himself by the highest spiritual laws with the Consciousness of God.

It may be argued that since Jesus was Divinely ordained, Divinely conceived, and Divinely born, and predetermined to be the *Son of God* and the Saviour of the world, that no earthly power and certainly no earthly Council could either grant or fail to grant Him the privilege of such attunement with the Consciousness of God. This is unquestionably true, and nowhere in the records with which I am dealing, and nowhere in the presentday teachings of the Rosicrucians, is it intimated that if Jesus had not passed through the preparation and experiences outlined by the Great White Brotherhood, He would have been unable to attune Himself just as completely with the Divine Consciousness, or become conscious of the Godhood or Christhood within Him. From the very hour of His birth all of the *Magi*, wise men, High Priests, and most learned advisers of the Brotherhood were His inferiors in Divine attunement and soul preparation for the great mission. It was no presumption on the part of these great men to perform their time-honored duty of accepting Joseph as a Neophyte and giving Him every one of the tests and trials and offering Him every opportunity for development as had been offered to the greatest among them. Nor did Joseph Himself consider the attitude assumed by the Brotherhood in treating Him as a Neophyte, and as one who had to be prepared, a failure of recognition, on their part, of His superior position among them. We shall see later on that even after Joseph had completed all the preparation that the Brotherhood prescribed for Him, and they had acknowledged Him ready for His mission in life, He *voluntarily offered Himself* for a final act of preparation in the knowledge that all these things were necessary for the work He desired to accomplish, and which had been Cosmically planned for Him.

Naturally, I wish it were possible for me to outline here the further initiations, ceremonies, and steps of preparation through which Joseph passed during the years in which He remained in Egypt. These things are never revealed to those who are not high initiates of the Brotherhood; and Jesus Himself, during his entire mission, revealed them to no one but His Apostles whom He carefully selected and Whom He constituted as His sacred council, and initiated as He had been initiated. I hardly think that any of my readers expect these things to be published in any book of this kind, nor in any book for the general public; and I am sure that the most learned and reasonable of my readers would doubt the authenticity of any printed record which claimed to contain such details.

It is possible, however, to speak of the last and final stage of His preparation for the ministry, which was held in the chambers of the Great Pyramid now known as the pyramid of Cheops.

Much has been said in various books and magazine articles in recent years about the chambers and secret rooms of the Great Pyramid, and space in this volume does not permit even a brief explanation of the intricate arrangement of the passageways and ancient chambers that are built within and beneath this great structure. The average tourist to Egypt sees the several pyramids that are grouped almost as a unit just outside of Cairo and close to the famous Sphinx. These tourists are generally told that the Pyramid was built as a tomb, and that it is a solid structure built over a burial chamber. Even the most ingenious of the guides who escort the tourists to the Pyramids refuse to admit that there are secret chambers and ceremonial rooms within this unique building. However, during my recent visit to the Pyramid, and while in the company of several high officers of the Rosicrucian Order of Egypt and a number of officers of the Order in America, we were permitted to enter these secret rooms and to verify the facts contained in our records.

It may be surprising to my readers to know that in the ancient times, or in the times with which we are dealing, the entrance way to the principal ceremonial rooms of the Pyramid was not through any doorway in the Pyramid itself, but through a secret passageway built between the two huge paws of the Sphinx. These paws rest upon a high foundation wall, forming two sides of a court in front of the Sphinx, in the center of which stood an altar. Back of this altar, still partly in ruins, and just beneath the breast of the Sphinx, was the secret doorway, well guarded, opening only by application of certain secret contrivances which only a few knew, that led to long subterranean passageways under the Sphinx, under the sands, and the foundation walls of the Pyramid, and to the great reception hall far below the surface surrounding the Pyramid. It was to the outer court in front of the Sphinx that the Neo-phytes who were well-prepared and deemed worthy of the secret of the entrance way to the Pyramids were brought and given their first induction into the mys-teries of the higher degrees. Such ceremonies usually occurred at midnight, when the Neophytes and the few who conducted the outer-court ceremony wended their way separately to this sacred spot, guarded and pro-tected by trusted brethren who remained at distant points from the Sphinx and the Pyramid as watchers and sentinels. Only those who once actually passed

This symbol is called in Christian mysticism the "Monogram of Christ." It is often used also as a symbol of Christianity. The author of this book traced this monogram on the face of a number of the tombs in the Catacombs at Rome, and in some of the ancient carvings of Egypt. Early Christian missionaries were misled by the discovery of this symbol in foreign lands, and believed it indicated the presence of earlier Christian missionaries. The symbol was in use long before Christianity adopted it. It was the original monogram of Osiris. The sacred banner of Constantine called the "Labarum" on which was placed the sign by which he was to conquer was inscribed with the sacred monogram shown above. It was also the mystical sign of Jupiter Ammon. The monogram had a mystical origin in the mystery teachings of the Brotherhood of Egypt, and it has been found engraved on a medal of Ptolemy, King of Cyrene. An identical monogram was also found on the coins of Herod the Great, issued before the Christian Era. The Roman Catholic Encyclopedia claims that the X and the P are the first two letters of a Greek word meaning "Christ." This authority also admits that the monogram was also used in pre-Christian periods as a mystical emblem. The monogram composed of X. P. N. is another symbol of the title, "Our Lord Jesus Christ."

through the ceremony within the Pyramid knew of the secret entrance way and the existence of the rooms and passageways.

Joseph was brought before the outer court of the Sphinx and clothed in purple robes during the preliminary ceremony held at midnight. At the completion of the ceremony, He was escorted through the subterranean passageway to the reception room beneath the Pyramid. After further ceremony here in this room, the sublime ceremony of being raised to the highest pinnacle of initiation began. This was performed by escorting Joseph up various inclines to the several different levels within the Pyramid, on each of which was a small chamber. After having reached the highest of these chambers, practically in the center of the Pyramid, the final ceremony took place. During this the royal diadem was placed upon the head of Joseph, indicating that He was no longer a Neophyte, nor even a peer among the Masters of the Brotherhood, but the greatest of them all. For over an hour a pontifical ceremony was conducted, culminating in a period of silence and meditation while Joseph knelt before the altar. Then a great light filled the chamber, which was otherwise lighted only by candles and three torches. A white dove descended in the light and rested on the head of Joseph while the Hierophant rose, and various bells in the chambers beneath began pealing the great announcement to the world. A slight figure rising behind the Hierophant like an angelic being, commanded

Joseph to rise while the voice of this being proclaimed: "This is Jesus the Christ; arise!" And all within the chamber united in saying "Amen."

The symbol shown above is often called the Crucified Serpent. We find in many ancient records a cross of this kind with either a dove, a rose, the sun, or the serpent on it. The serpentine crucifix represented in the ancient symbolism the sun after it had lost its power. In some mystical writings it was used as an emblem of the crucifixion of the Christ to indicate that through such crucifixion the Son had lost His Divine Power.

The foregoing is but a very brief, greatly condensed outline of the final ceremony. The complete details present one of the most picturesque and elaborate set-tings ever recorded in the secret writings of the Brother-hood, and it is known that no such ceremony has ever occurred since then.

As the ceremony ended the officers and members of the high Council surrounded Joseph, who had now *attained* the name *Jesus* and had been acknowledged the Christ, and paid homage to Him and proclaimed Him the incarnation of the *Word,* or "the Living Logos." Then followed the ceremonial march to the chambers below, where the first of the Lord's *Suppers* was held as a symbolical feast.

Messengers were sent the next day, in all directions from Egypt to every land in which branches of the Brotherhood were located, to proclaim the coming of the Saviour and the announcement of His mission of redemption. Among these was one John from the Essene Brotherhood in Palestine, who had been a student at the schools in Egypt, preparing for his mission in life. He was known to be the reincarnation of Elijah, and he was sent to Palestine, the land in which, as Elijah, he had once before served as an Avatar and had attended the monastery at Carmel. It was his mission, like that of the other messengers sent to other lands, to proclaim the coming of the *Christ.*

And so all the peoples who were ready for the coming of the Lord were duly notified, and the great work of *Jesus the Christ* began.

CHAPTER XIII

THE MYSTIC BEGINNING OF
CHRIST'S MISSION

▽

HEN John reached Palestine he appeared in
public in the most humble clothing and with
great humility. His work was to announce
among the lowly and the humble in spirit the
coming of the great Redeemer. He presented
an entirely new idea inasmuch as he preached the doctrine of baptism for *redemption* or *regeneration.*

It may not be out of place here to state that Baptism
or the immersion in water and the use of water for
purification in a symbolical or Cosmic sense, was introduced into the rites and ceremonies of the Great White
Brotherhood in Egypt by one who was known as El-
Moria. He was one of the great Avatars in the early
days of the Brotherhood, and learned through meditation and Cosmic Illumination that water would cleanse
in a Cosmic sense as well as in a physical sense. It was
through his learned discussions before the High Council
of the Brotherhood in this regard that pools of purified
water were introduced in front of every altar in the
mystery temples of Egypt and other lands. It was this
same great Avatar who first introduced public Baptism
for spiritual regeneration by holding such ceremonies at
Lake Moeris, in the Fayuum district of Egypt, around

which centered one of the earliest of the advanced civilizations of Egypt.

Recently I made a trip to this place in company with others of our Brotherhood, and there saw the beautiful lake which is still a mystery to those who have tried to discover the source of its beautiful water, far from the Nile and in the very heart of desert lands. Here many of us re-enacted in the utmost sublimity the early form of Baptism, and symbolically celebrated the ancient rite. According to the records of the Rosicrucian Brotherhood, this is the first time that scores of men and women united in one reverential party participated in this ceremonial rite since the days before Christ, and of course it was the first time in the history of the world that such a group of persons from *America* ever re-ceived Baptism at the shore of Lake Moeris. For hun-dreds of years this beautiful lake has been unvisited by European or American tourists, and for a thousand years its history and its connection with the Christian rite of Baptism has remained unknown except to those in the Rosicrucian Order and those in the high branches of the Brotherhood in Tibet, India, and Egypt.

John was looked upon by the Jewish people as one of the sturdy race of Judah. Coming from the wilderness into their midst in pious clothing, they looked upon him as an ascetic. His camel's hair cloak was a symbol of penitence, and his words were those of an ancient prophet. John picked out the banks of the Jordan as his special territory for the work he wished to do. Appealing, as he intended, to the lowly and the humble, he attracted the attention of multitudes, which seemed to drink in his words and find hope in his proclamations. In selecting the valley of the Jordan he had chosen a place that seemed to be separated from the rest of the world, and filled with terrifying contrasts to the rest of Palestine. Around about was the rough land of volcanic formation and volcanic destruction. In fact, the part of the shores selected by John was known as the *Sea of Solitude,* but it was here that the Essenes had originally held such wonderful ceremonies and had es- tablished one of their first communities. It was truly Holy ground to John.

John's message was that which most of the Jews had hoped to hear in their lifetimes—the coming of the Messiah. But he warned them that they must prepare for His coming and prepare for it in a true spirit of repentance. His earnestness and the power with which He proclaimed that only the repentant, the purified, and those who were purged of all sin would see the Messiah, shocked the holy ones and antagonized the strictly orthodox.

From all parts of Palestine came those who wanted to hear the message of John, and witness his strange ceremonies in the waters of the river. About this time word came from other lands that other prophets were foretelling the coming of the Messiah. Over and over was repeated the ancient prophecy that *out of the land of Egypt would come the Son of God.*

Camps were built around the lake where earnest souls remained for weeks, many of them hoping that the Messiah would appear in the midst of the thousands who gathered there on feast days. A number asked permission to form a group to take up the work of John and to serve under him in the beginning of a *holy war*. Rumors of this plan reached the rulers of Palestine, and the priests at Jerusalem began to feel uneasy at the excitement of the populace. Other conditions in Pales' tine seemed to indicate that a great crisis was at hand. Tiberius, now seventy-four years of age, was indulging in such debauchery at Capri as was rapidly hastening his transition. Pontius Pilate was continuing his perse' cution of the Jews and becoming more furious.

It was in the midst of these conditions that Jesus the Christ quietly and without recognition returned to Galilee and greeted His mother, brothers and sisters in their little home, and awaited patiently the hour when the first message was to be given. To Jesus came the reports of the work being done by John, and how John was insisting that all who were worthy of regeneration and redemption must be Baptized by water. Finally Jesus decided that He should set the great example among the Gentiles of Galilee, and proceeded to the Jordan and submit Himself to John's Baptism. And so it was that Jesus entered the throngs of those standing by the shores of the Jordan listening to the preachments of John. Here He heard the voice of John thundering, "Repent ye, prepare ye the way of the Lord, make His path straight." As he baptized each applicant, he made his famous prophecy of the coming of the Messiah, saying: "I baptize you with water only, but He will baptize you with fire."

Jesus stepped forward and He and John faced each other for the first time since they had met in one of the conclaves in Egypt. Instantly John knew that he was in the presence of the Christ, and he folded his arms across his chest with the right hand over his heart, and the left hand over his right breast, making the salutation common among the Essenes, and Jesus replied by mak-ing a similar sign. Words passed between John and Jesus which have been variously recorded, but which constituted the formal recognition on the part of John that was due the great Master before him. Then Jesus stepped into the water and submitted *voluntarily* to the baptism. As stated in the preceding chapter, this act clearly shows that Jesus recognized the necessity of formal preparation and ceremonial procedure, even though He knew of the Divine, Cosmic appointment of His Messiahship.

It is one of the important doctrines of the Great White Brotherhood that spiritual illumination and Cos-mic Consciousness enter the being of man only *after* he is ready. There is an ancient belief based upon the mystic teachings of the Orient that *when each indi-vidual is ready for the coming of the Master*, who is to guide and instruct him in the higher things of life, *the Master will appear*. But the emphasis here should be placed upon readiness, which includes worthiness and sincerity of purpose. Unless one is truly ready and properly prepared by *instruction, guidance, and the help that lies in the process based upon spiritual laws*, no Master will appear, no bursting of inner Cosmic Consciousness will become manifest, and no great Illumination of transcendental light will come. Worthiness must be *attained*, preparedness made manifest, and readiness earned by *voluntary* effort.

Just as John was sent ahead to prepare the way, just as the great Avatars of the past found it necessary to preach and teach in order to prepare the many for spiritual regeneration, and just as Jesus taught His disciples and hosts of others that they might mentally comprehend and spiritually apprehend the laws and principles leading to spiritual awakening, so have the teachers and Masters in the mystery schools of the Brotherhood in all lands maintained the systems of instruction and methods of preparation that have proved to be adequate and efficient. The seeker for Divine effulgence and Cosmic Consciousness who attempts to await the coming of the Master and the brightness of Illumination *without study and preparation, and without association with those who are likewise qualified to aid and assist*, delays the coming of the great day and often closes the door to the coming of the Master. It is in this fact that we find warrant for the establishment of the churches and for the maintenance of the secret

J H S

Another monogram for Christ is that formed of three letters, supposed to be the first two and last letters of the Greek word for "Jesus," but the last letter was finally changed to the Latin letter "S" so that the I. H. S. stood for "Jesus, Hominum, Salvator"—"Jesus, the Saviour of Man." The letters were also used to mean "In Hoc Salus" and "In Hoc Signo," meaning "In this Cross, is Salvation," or "By This Sign, Conquer." The I and J in the early Latin language were identical in form, and in the early monograms composed of the letters I. H. S., the mark of abbreviation was put above the letters. These abbreviation marks were later misunderstood or so crudely carved that they were considered to be a cross over the H, and in this wise a new monogram was evolved appearing as shown above, with the cross resting on the letter H. This monogram is now the official emblem as adopted by the Jesuits.

brotherhoods and societies devoted to the spiritual preparation of man.

So Jesus entered the water and immersed His body in it, while John stood by ready to give Him humble benediction. As Jesus rose erectly in the water, and before John could speak, a great light came down from the heavens and surrounded Jesus and remained with Him as a magnificent, blinding aura of iridescent illumination. John stepped back, more in fear of the brilliancy of the light than through astonishment, and the multitudes stood aghast, speechless, and spellbound by the sight before their eyes. Then from out of the heavens there descended a great, white, luminous dove, as bright as molten silver, and as magnificent as the spiritual light which surrounded the body of Christ. The dove lighted upon the shoulder of Jesus, and while all stood silent and motionless, a voice came from the center of their attention, melodious but resounding like a trumpet call, proclaiming: "This is my beloved Son!" John knew, as did the other Essenes who were assembled there, that the Holy Ghost had descended upon Jesus as it had descended upon Mary, and had created in Him a new being—the Divine being of Christhood and Sonship *with* God—as it had created in Mary a new being and a Sonship *of* God.

CHAPTER XIV

HIS REAL DOCTRINES AND MIRACLES

▽

HE whole public life of Jesus, from the time of His baptism up to and including the cruci' fixion, was an outer, objective manifestation of the series of initiations through which He had passed secretly—or more or less subjec' tively—during His years of preparation. This impor' tant fact is often overlooked by those who are analytical students of His mission and life work, and is certainly slighted in emphasis by those who attempt to interpret His doctrines, teachings, activities, sufferings, trials, vic' tories, and defeats.

I have intimated in many places, in the preceding chapters, that the fundamental mysticism of Christi' anity has been unwarrantedly neglected by modern Christianity and churchanity, but is being re'introduced into Christianity by the foremost theologians and clergy' men. At a recent conclave of one of the high Protestant churches of America and England, the statement was made by one of the foremost ecclesiastical authorities that the salvation of the Christian church today de' pended upon the proper emphasis of the mystical foun' dation of Christianity.

Pristine Christianity was intended to carry on the teachings and doctrines revealed by Jesus the Christ, and these were highly mystical though reduced to worldly parables. The Apostles of Jesus, who were carefully selected by Him because of their previous experience in life and their worthiness, were carefully initiated by Him and spiritually developed during the secret conclaves which He held, and which never became a part of the public records of His life. The work that these Apostles carried on, and which was later taken up by the Holy Fathers of the Christian church, was dual in nature. There was the secret or *inner circle* of students of Christianity, who were gradually developed in the mystical principles involved in the doctrines revealed by Jesus; and there was the *outer circle* which heard only the parables and preachments given to the multitudes by Jesus and amplified by His followers.

For many centuries after the life of Jesus the early *Christian Church* was more of a secret mystery school than a public place or system of general religious worship. It was not until the conclaves of the Holy Fathers in the fourth, fifth, sixth, and seventh centuries, that the present-day system of churchanity, separate from mystical Christianity, was adopted. And even so, the few in every land who were deemed worthy and properly qualified were permitted to enter the little known *inner circle* and bask in the brilliant light of transcendental illumination. That the outer circle, with its churchanity, had a glorious work to do is unquestionable, and I do not mean to criticize the plans which permitted the outer work to grow with greater strength or to a more enlarged form than the work of the inner circle. Even today the proportion of those who are ready to enter the inner circle is so small compared with those who are only partially ready for the broader and more general work of the outer circle, that it often seems like a hopeless task to make the inner circle suffi-ciently large enough to carry on the great work that must be carried on to retain the mystical elements of Christianity for future development. I cannot agree altogether with those who criticize the church and claim that *system* and organization have eaten away the heart of Christianity, or that outer pomp and ceremony, structure, and operations, have denied any place at all to the mystical work of the inner chamber. Spiritual development is a matter of evolution, and progressive evolution is rapid only with the few. The greatest work must be among the masses in order that the occasional one in every thousand persons may find the *Path* that leads to the inner circle.

Before Jesus could begin His great work in life, and before He could lay the foundation of this work by the establishment of His personal school and personal coun-cil, composed of selected Neophytes who would be His trusted Apostles, He had to face once again the tests and trials of higher initiation. This time, however, He would not approach these things as a *Neophyte*, but as the ordained *Christ*. And since his work would be in the objective world, so would His tests, trials, and initiatory experiences be of the objective world. For this reason, we see why it was that the first incident of His public career was His retirement into the silence for meditation.

In a previous part of this book I have referred to this principle of *entering the silence* and have commented upon the benefits of silent meditation. In the Books of Matthew, Mark, and Luke, of the Christian Bible, we find reference to Jesus entering the silence, or going into the wilderness, whereas nothing is said of it in the Book of John. John was the most mystical of the writers of the New Testament, and His gospel emphasizes more of the mystical principles of Christianity than any of the others. His reason for skipping over the incidents of Jesus' meditation in the wilderness is probably because of its personal nature, and because it had no bearing upon the work of Jesus with the public.

Throughout the Christian Bible we find so many references in both the Old and New Testaments regarding those who went up on a mountain for illumination or for intimate contact with God or God's Consciousness. The proof that these references to *mountains* of *inspiration* or *mountains* of illumination have not been considered in their true mystical light is found in the fact that expeditions composed of scientists and ecclesiastical authorities have sought for many of these "mountains" in the Holy Land, and have labored diligently to select the proper one to fit the various incidents described in the Bible. In many cases, the "mountains" selected have proved to be mere hills, much like thousands of others to be found in such a rolling country; and surprise has been expressed by a great many that such places should have been called "mountains" at all. The truth of the matter is that *going up onto a mountain for illumination* is a symbolical, mystical statement, indicating no actual, physical mountain, and referring to no physical height at all. We are surprised to find that the ancients who lived in lands where there were no mountains or even large hills, referred, in their writings, to the illuminations which they received upon *mountain* tops. Even some of the early Christians in Egypt spoke of the illumination which came to them out in the desert on the mountain top. Going up *onto a mountain* meant, in the mystical terminology of the Great White Brotherhood, and in all of the mystical writings of the Avatars and Masters of the past, the raising of one's inner spiritual self to a great height where Cosmic contact, or Cosmic Consciousness, was definite and complete. We find that all such experiences in the Old Testament, including the one regarding Moses and the spiritual contact he made with God, were for the purpose of attaining spiritual illumination or the development and test of some spiritual principle. Logically, the very opposite of this expression was also true. Whenever one of the great mystics or Masters of the past had to contact or come in contest with one of the earthly, non-spiritual phases of life and wrestle with a problem that was purely worldly, he went into the *valley* or into the *wilderness,* and not to the mountain top.

Thus we see why the first incident of the life of Jesus, which concerned objective principles and earthly trials and tribulations, took Him into the desert wilder-ness instead of onto a mountain top. We read in the Christian writings that He spent forty days and forty nights in this wilderness. During this time He fasted and hungered, and in other ways suffered the conditions of the body and flesh.

It is interesting to note that the numbers *seven* and *forty* are the numbers mostly used in mystical literature, because they have a mystical significance. I will not take the time to recall, to my readers, the number of times the number *seven* is used in the Old and New Testament, beginning with the creation of the world and the number of days in the week, and the fact that the *seventh* day was made the Holy day! for I am sure that a few minutes' reflection will bring to mind many such uses of this symbolical number. The number *forty* is used so many times that its significance becomes ap-parent, even to the casual student of the Bible. It is found very frequently in the most ancient of sacred writings in many lands. The Egyptians claimed that the body was not completely freed of the soul until after *forty* days of preparation. Moses abstained from bread and water for *forty* days and *forty* nights, during his period of Cosmic contact. Moses was on the mount for *forty* days and *forty* nights; and was on Mount Sinai

THE MYSTICAL LIFE OF JESUS

the second time for *forty* days and *forty* nights. The men who went to Canaan were *forty* days on their spiritual journey. It was prophesied that no foot of man or beast would pass through Egypt for *forty* years.

Elijah was *forty* days and *forty* nights on Mount Horab, and was the same number of days and nights on Mount Carmel. The children of Israel were in the hands of the Philistines for *forty* years; and for *forty* years, the children of Israel ate manna. The people of Ninevah had to repent for *forty* days. We find that Saul, David, Solomon, and Joash reigned as kings for *forty* years. So we should not be surprised to find that Jesus went into the wilderness for *forty* days and *forty* nights.

We must also remember that both Moses and Elijah began their public ministrations by fasting for *forty* days and *forty* nights, and preparing for their final acts. In the case of Jesus, however, His first acts were to be those dealing with material, earthly affairs, while with Moses and Elijah they were to be of a spiritual nature, dealing with spiritual problems. Hence, Jesus went into the lowlands of a wilderness while Moses and Elijah went up on the mountain top.

We find from the Christian accounts of the experiences of Jesus during His *forty* days in the wilderness that it was a period of temptation, and the story being told symbolically, the temptations of the earth are personified as coming from the person of Satan. The temptations, however, through which Jesus had to pass were symbolical of those presented to Him during His initiation in Egypt, when He was being prepared for the ministry. According to the old records Jesus Himself meditated upon what form of temptations the world would present to Him during His ministry, and one by one these temptations were stated by Himself as though being spoken by the "tempter." Then He reviewed the nature of the temptation, analyzed it carefully, and formulated what answer He would be able to give and what attitude He would be able to maintain throughout His life, if ever brought face to face with such temptations. Therefore, the entire process was one of self-examination; and it is recorded that the ultimate result of the self-examination, and a consideration of the conditions that Jesus would have to face brought Him to the point where He realized that He would come to the final close of His career during a public attack upon His methods and life, culminating in His crucifixion. Therefore, we understand why Jesus made prophetic reference, a number of times, to the sad close of His life, and why He anticipated and was more or less prepared for what actually occurred. In truth, He knew that He would not be the first of the Avatars who had been crucified, and who had been accused wrongly by the very people who would have benefited the most from the instructions and teachings offered.

In fact, we find that as soon as Jesus had completed His forty days of meditation and self-examination, and had outlined His plans for His ministry, He learned